A Guide to the Notorious Bars of Alaska

3rd Edition

Doug Vandegraft

KENMORE, WA

6524 NE 181st St., Suite 2, Kenmore, WA 98028

Epicenter Press is a regional press publishing nonfiction books about the arts, history, environment, and diverse cultures and lifestyles of Alaska and the Pacific Northwest. For more information, visit www.EpicenterPress.com

A Guide to the Notorious Bars of Alaska, 3rd Edition
Copyright © 2025 by Doug Vandegraft

All rights reserved. No part of this publication may be reproduced, stored in a retrieval system, or transmitted in any form by any means, electronic, mechanical, photocopying, recording, or otherwise, without the prior written permission of the publisher. Permission is given for brief excerpts to be published with book reviews in newspaper, magazines, newsletters, catalogs, and online publications.

Library of Congress Control Number: 2024940298

ISBN: 978-1-684922-32-1 (Trade Paperback)
ISBN: 978-1-684922-33-8 (Ebook)

Front cover photo: *Interior of a saloon in Wrangell, circa 1898. Photo by Otto D. Goetze. Used by permission of the Washington State Historical Society: 1969.8.2.7 This is possibly the Red Light Club Room, which was at 516 Front Street. All saloons were illegal in Alaska until July 1, 1899.*

Back cover photo: *Exterior of the Bird House Bar, Indian, in 1988. The Bird House burned down in 1996. The author is at center; his brother Mark Vandegraft at right; friend Steve Hill at left.*

Cover design: Scott Book
Interior design: Melissa Vail Coffman

Gary Nichols at the Sportsman's Inn, Whittier, Alaska (2000).

*This book is dedicated to Gary Nichols
(aka "Stout" aka "The King") 1957 – 2004*

CONTENTS

Preface vii
Introduction ix
    Why I Wrote This Book x
    What Makes a Bar Notorious xi
In Search of Alaska's Oldest Bars xiii
How This Book Is Organized xiv
A Short History of Alcohol and Bars in Alaska xvii
    Russian Period: 1741 – 1867 xvii
    First Prohibition: 1867 – 1899 xviii
    Liquor Becomes Legal: 1899 – 1917 xix
    Second Prohibition: 1918 – 1933 xxi
    End of the 'Bone-Dry' Law: 1933 xxii
    Dispensaries to Cocktail Bars: 1934 – 1940 xxiii
    WWII and Statehood: 1941 – 1959 xxiii
    Oil, areas of prohibition, and tourism: 1960 – present day xxiv
Notorious Bars of
    Southeast Alaska 1
    Southcentral Alaska 57
    Interior Alaska 161
    Southwest Alaska 199
    Western Alaska 225
Acknowledgements 243
Iindex of Notorious Bars 247

"Research is never completed. Around the corner lurks another opportunity of interview, another book to read, a courthouse to explore, a document to verify."

—Catherine Drinker Bowen

PREFACE

THIS BOOK WAS FIRST PUBLISHED in 2014 and was revised in 2017. I was working on the third edition in late 2019. Like most of us, I learned of the outbreak of COVID-19 in early 2020. Later that year, I received an email from Lael Morgan, my publisher, who made a prediction about bars in Alaska. "I think it's going to take more than just a few months to find out who will survive the pandemic." She was right, of course.

The pandemic was brutal to restaurants and bars around the world. In Alaska, non-essential businesses were ordered to close for indoor service. After those businesses were allowed to open, social distancing and masking policies made visiting a bar an exercise in compromise.

I resumed working on the third edition of Notorious in the fall of 2023 and started counting the bars from the second edition that had closed. I was only half-surprised at the nineteen bars that made the "gone" list: First City Saloon, Ketchikan; Rendezvous, Juneau; Hideaway Club and Carpentier's Cocktail Lounge, Anchorage; The Pit, Seward; The Albatross, Kenai; Lamplight Bar, Nikiski; Fat Albert's Tavern, Beluga; Cordova Hotel Bar and Anchor Bar, Cordova; Club Alaskan and Club Manchu, Fairbanks; Dew Drop

Inn, Anderson; Refinery Lounge and Moose Creek Lodge, North Pole; Big D Bar, Big Delta; McGuire's Tavern, McGrath; Polaris Bar and Anchor Tavern, Nome.

As per my policy, I will reflect these nineteen bars on my website in the *Bars of Alaska's Past* pages (www.notoriousbarsofak.com). A few of them are not actually gone but have morphed into a completely different bar in name and character (i.e. Club Alaskan in Fairbanks and Refinery Lounge in North Pole).

Notorious (historic) bars of Alaska continue to be an endangered species. Only eight bars from the first edition had closed when the second edition was published. As was the case then, some of the nineteen bars were just barely hanging on, and the pandemic was the final nail in the coffin. However, the bars that did survive made the most of their downtime by making improvements, replacing furniture and fixtures, fixing sinks and toilets, and giving the bar the most thorough cleaning it had ever had.

I am happy to report that I have added seventeen bars to this edition, including a gay bar (Mad Myrna's in Anchorage) and a sports bar (Eddie's Sports Bar in Anchorage). Others have now met my twenty-five years in business requirement (Hole in the Wall in Ketchikan; Bernie's Bungalow in Anchorage; Birchwood Saloon in Chugiak). And others should have been included in past editions (Craig Inn in Craig; The Sandbar and Squirez in Juneau; JJ's Lounge and The Avenue in Anchorage, 4 Royle Parkers in Soldotna; The Place in Kenai; Moosehead Saloon in Palmer; Silver Fox Inn in Wasilla; Pioneer Lodge in Willow; and the Talkeetna Inn in Talkeetna). Also, the Carousel Lounge in Anchorage had closed when the second edition was published but has since reopened.

Sadly, Lael Morgan, my friend and mentor, passed away in 2022. I was lucky to meet her when I did. As per the example she set, I will continue to strive for my research to be accurate, and my writing to be entertaining.

INTRODUCTION

I MOVED TO ANCHORAGE, ALASKA, in August 1983 from Flagstaff, Arizona, where I had graduated from college the year before. I was twenty-four years old and had accepted a job as a cartographer with the federal government. I had never been to Alaska and I was in awe not only of the scenery, but also of the city that would become my home for the next seventeen years. Anchorage was still booming from the billions of dollars of revenue generated by the Prudhoe Bay oilfields and the completion of the trans-Alaska oil pipeline. Construction of homes and commercial buildings was happening all over town. Anyone wanting a job could find one and the pay was considerably more compared to a similar job in the Lower 48 states.

 I discovered quickly that Alaskans not only work hard but love to play hard. Being of an age when going to a bar was still a novelty, I was impressed by the large number of bars and by the very liberal laws (compared to Arizona) that were in place at the time. Bars stayed open until 5 a.m. and then reopened at 6 a.m. Happy Hour specials included deals such as "dime beer" and fifty-cent well drinks. You could buy six drinks at a time, called a "six pack." Live music, including rock, country, jazz, and reggae was featured at many of these places. Recreational drugs were also very available, both in the bars as well as on the streets. A walk along Fourth Avenue or Spenard Road, regardless of the season or the time of day, could put you in contact with drug dealers and an incredible number of hookers. I felt like I had moved to a twentieth century version of the wild, wild, west!

The crazy '80s didn't last, of course. Tony Knowles, then Mayor of Anchorage, and the Mothers Against Drunk Driving organization, got laws passed that outlawed happy hours, forced the bars to close at 2:30 a.m., and chased the hookers off the streets. Many of the bars I frequented, such as the Midnight Express and Spenardo DaVinci's, eventually closed their doors as the economy first normalized and then crashed in the late '80s. Other bars, such as the Panhandle, the Cabin Tavern, and Chilkoot Charlie's continued to thrive despite changes to the laws and the economy.

I had originally planned to live in Alaska for three to five years, but I found myself falling in love with the incredible geography, culture, and lifestyle that is uniquely Alaskan. Partly because of my job, and because of my love of camping and fishing, I began travelling to communities throughout the state. In every town or village, I made it a point to seek out the local watering holes.

Why I Wrote This Book

AS I GREW OLDER AND visited other parts of the United States, I began to realize the uniqueness of the bars of Alaska. I had never seen a bar anywhere else that looked like (or smelled like) the Bird House on Turnagain Arm, with its permanently slanted bar, and walls covered with bras, panties, photos and business cards. There were other Salty Dog bars in the Lower 48, but none had the personality or atmosphere of the Salty Dawg Saloon located at the end of the Homer Spit. When I first travelled to Dutch Harbor in the Aleutian Islands on a work assignment, I couldn't wait to stop in at the Elbow Room, the bar that all commercial fishermen talked about. For years I had heard stories about Rose's bar in Pelican, a remote town in southeast Alaska. Rose's is an establishment that the Alaska Alcoholic Beverage Control Board used the word "notorious" to describe. What a treat it was to visit this famous bar and talk to Rose Miller!

I have always loved history, and when I visited a bar, I eventually began asking historical questions about the bar owners, managers and patrons. My standard lead-off question was "How long has this bar been here?" followed by "Has it always been in this same location?" and "Is the (name of bar) famous for something?"

A visit from a high school buddy in 1999 spawned the idea of writing this book. We were discussing Alaska bars and I was telling him the kinds of facts I had learned, such as: there are many bars in Alaska that are operating under the same name and at the same location as when they opened their doors after prohibition ended in 1933; that many Alaska bars are internationally famous for their unique locations and/or outrageous reputations; that many Alaska bars double as community centers—and occasionally even churches! We both agreed that a guidebook should be written that would celebrate the famous and historic bars of Alaska. We also thought that using the word notorious would be applicable and would help create a catchy title.

What Makes a Bar Notorious

THE IDEA THAT A DRINKING establishment is not only famous but notorious is not unique to Alaska. Bars such as Gadsby's Tavern in Alexandria, Virginia, the White Horse Tavern in Boston, Massachusetts, or McSorley's Old Ale House in New York City have been around for so long that their histories speak volumes about the people and the events that have shaped the United States. When a bar is around for more than twenty-five years it tends to gain a reputation and a kind of notoriety. This is especially true for the bars of Alaska. For example, the Board of Trade in Nome was serving drinks in 1900 when the gold rush was in full force. And despite being prohibited from selling alcohol during prohibition, the Board of Trade continues to remind us today of a time when the "City of Golden Sands" was home to more than ten thousand people.

Bars are usually the scene of celebratory events, such as wedding receptions, anniversaries, bachelor and bachelorette parties, promotions, bar mitzvahs, and of course birthday parties. Many bars have become popular as places to enjoy live music or to watch sporting events. Unfortunately, bars can also be the scene of tragedy, sometimes in the form of violence and even murder. As I have discovered through my research, when a bar is mentioned in a local newspaper, it is often the "police blotter" section of the paper. This is certainly not true of all bars in Alaska. However, I believe that a significant event or occurrence at a particular location, be it wonderful or tragic, will help us remember that place. In time, these memories seem to grow in impact. The facts get distorted, and the legend grows. Before long, that place becomes synonymous with the stories, and ultimately becomes notorious.

In determining the criteria that would qualify a bar as notorious, and for inclusion in this book, I decided on the following:

1. Bar must be in continuous operation for at least 25 years.

2. Bar must remain located in the same city, town, or village.

3. The name of the bar must remain the same—or—it is still known by the former name.

Any bar that possesses these qualities will certainly be well known and have gained notoriety within its home community, and within the state. As the reader will see, I have remained rigid in adhering to the criteria, allowing for just a few exceptions. I have also tended to focus on those establishments which are primarily bars, and not restaurants.

To clarify this last point, I define a restaurant as an establishment that has a major focus on feeding people. In most cases it takes reservations and has a hostess who greets and seats you. This definition means that the reader will not find some very popular places in this book, such as The Hangar in Juneau, the Peanut Farm in Anchorage, and Pike's Landing in Fairbanks.

In Search of Alaska's Oldest Bars

THE QUESTION OF HOW OLD a bar is has posed more than one challenge to my research. The Imperial Bar in Juneau advertises itself as the oldest bar in Alaska (it probably is). The Imperial points out that it was once known as the Missouri and then the Louvre, and was doing business back in the 1880s. However, the bar was not in the business of selling alcoholic beverages, at least not legally, during the almost fifteen years of prohibition (1918 – 1933). For the purposes of this book, I consider the period of the most recent prohibition as having effectively reset the clock as to how old a bar can be. Therefore, the earliest date a bar in Alaska could have been issued a license is April 7, 1933, the day that beer and wine were once again legal to sell.

The 1933 liquor license records for Alaska are scant. The National Archives in Seattle has them, but only for Southeast Alaska. The territorial liquor license records from the 1940s through the 1960s reside at the State Archives in Juneau. These records have provided me with some of the most accurate accounting of when a bar received their first liquor license. The 1934 – 1935 *Alaska Directory and Gazetteer* and the 1945 *Alaska Business Directory* also provided useful information. The digitizing of several Alaska newspapers in recent years has enabled me to quickly find reliable information, particularly when they report the approval of local liquor licenses. Unfortunately for me, the "History of this License" document, found in the Alcoholic

Beverage Control (ABC) Board files, provides information no earlier than 1956. I have found advertisements in newspapers, announcing the "Grand Opening" of certain establishments, but grand openings aren't always reliable indicators as to the age of a bar, and sometimes are just celebrations of a recent remodel, change of management, or even a new bartender.

From my twenty-four years of research, I believe that the oldest bars in Alaska, in continuous operation since 1933 are:

- Imperial Bar, Juneau
- Pioneer Bar, Haines
- Alaskan Hotel Bar, Cordova
- Panhandle Bar, Anchorage
- Board of Trade Saloon, Nome
- International Bar, Fairbanks

How This Book Is Organized

I HAVE DIVIDED THIS BOOK into five distinct geographic regions of Alaska: Southeast, Southcentral, Interior, Southwest, and Western.

Southeast covers the Panhandle and Inside Passage towns, including Yakutat on the eastern Gulf Coast. Beginning in Ketchikan, towns are listed from south to north.

Southcentral encompasses the towns south of the Alaska Range, including all of Cook Inlet and Prince William Sound. Beginning in Anchorage, towns are listed as if you were driving south to the Kenai Peninsula, including a side trip to Whittier. Towns are then listed as if you were driving north on the Glenn Highway to the Richardson Highway, accessing Cordova via ferry from Valdez, and then north to Paxson. Towns are listed on the Parks Highway from Wasilla to Cantwell.

Interior covers the towns north of the Alaska Range. Beginning in Fairbanks, towns are listed as if you were driving south on the Parks Highway and then south on the Richardson and Alaska Highways, and east on the Taylor Highway. Towns are then listed as if you were driving north on the Steese and Elliott highways. Also included are the bush towns of Galena and McGrath.

Southwest encompasses the towns along the western Gulf of Alaska and those located on or adjacent to both sides of the Alaska Peninsula, including the Aleutian Islands and eastern Bristol Bay. Beginning in Kodiak, towns are listed traveling southwesterly.

Western includes towns along the Bering Sea Coast, including western Bristol Bay (Dillingham), the Seward Peninsula (Nome), and the Pribilof Islands (St. Paul)

Noticeably absent to readers familiar with Alaska geography is reference to the Arctic regions and the Yukon-Kuskokwim delta regions. Towns and villages in these areas, such as Kotzebue, Barrow, Kaktovik, Unalakleet, and Togiak have voted to prohibit the sale of alcohol.

I hope you enjoy these unique establishments as much as I do.

Cheers!

— Douglas L. Vandegraft

A SHORT HISTORY OF ALCOHOL AND BARS IN ALASKA

ALCOHOL HAS LONG BEEN A part of Alaskan culture, and Alaskans have a legendary thirst for alcoholic beverages. The remoteness of Alaska, seasonal darkness, isolation, and loneliness creates a tremendous need to socialize, which provides a unique niche for bars to prosper.

Russian Period: 1741 – 1867

THE RUSSIANS INTRODUCED LIQUOR TO the Aleuts (indigenous people of the Aleutian Islands, Alaska Natives) as early as 1741. The Russian-American Company, which operated out of Sitka beginning in 1808, sold its wares, including liquor, to whalers, fur traders, fish processors and prospectors. During the 1830s, rum, vodka, and brandy were routinely traded with the indigenous people for labor, furs, ivory, and physical affections.

First Prohibition: 1867 – 1899

THE UNITED STATES BOUGHT ALASKA from Russia in 1867, and the US Army was given jurisdiction to manage the new "territory." The Alaska Act of 1868 made it illegal to import liquor, and in 1873, Alaska was classified as "Indian country" which made it illegal to give or sell alcohol to any "Indian" or Alaska Native. Violators were to be brought before a judge within five days, which was next to impossible as the nearest civilian judge was in Oregon. Instead of enforcing the laws, the soldiers at Sitka taught Alaska Natives how to give a kick to a traditional beverage made of bark and berries by adding molasses and yeast for fermentation and then distilling the results. The first batch of this mind-numbing concoction known as "hoochinoo" (or simply "hooch") was reportedly made at the Tlingit village of Hootchenoo near present-day Angoon. The word 'hooch' is Alaska's contribution to the American vernacular, a term which is still in use today.

Because the liquor laws were not being enforced, saloons were operating in Sitka as early as 1869. The Sitka Saloon, Central Saloon, Caplan & Co., G.W. Brady's, and the One Bit House advertised openly in the *Alaska Times* newspaper and were probably some of the very first bars in Alaska.

The Organic Act of 1884 established a civil government for Alaska. The legislation provided Alaska with a governor, district judge, district attorney, one US Marshal and just four Deputy Marshals. The Act prohibited all alcohol except for medicinal and scientific purposes. Enforcement of the law was extremely challenging due to the lack of Marshals, funding, and transportation. This absence of resources reflects the political influence of commercial interests, most notably the Alaska Commercial Company, which had twenty-three trading posts along the coast, and used liquor for trade with the Alaska Natives and white populations.

The discovery of gold near present-day Juneau in 1880 and the Klondike gold rush of 1898 introduced Alaska to people all over the world. Thousands were coming via ships from Seattle and San Francisco to seek their fortunes. Newcomers found that saloons were operating openly in Wrangell, Juneau and Skagway. By this time, Congress finally realized that it was impossible to keep liquor out of Alaska.

Liquor Becomes Legal: 1899 – 1917

IN 1899, CONGRESS REPEALED ALASKA'S prohibition laws. Territorial Governor John G. Brady established a system of local option, licensed liquor sales. The licensee had to gain the approval of the majority of men and women living within two miles of the saloon. This is one of the first known examples of women being allowed to vote in the United States. Annual liquor license fees cost between five hundred dollars and two thousand dollars depending on the population of the town. The license fees were used to support schools and build court houses and jails. In some towns, the license fees funded the entire local government. The legality of liquor applied only to white residents; it remained illegal to supply liquor to Alaska Natives in or outside of a saloon. In fact, prohibition for Alaska Natives was not repealed until 1953.

On June 5, 1899, Peter Nelson received the very first "Barroom license" for his establishment at Sourdough Flats, a now-abandoned village on Unimak Island. The following year, W.Y. Egan received license No. 1 for his "Bar Room" in Tanana.

License No. 1 was issued to W.Y. Egan for a "Bar Room" in Tanana. Alaska State Archives

The price for drinks varied by location, but in general, draught beer sold for ten cents a glass while whiskey and mixed drinks sold for twenty-five cents a glass. The only women allowed in the saloons, other than prostitutes, were entertainers and "percentage girls." The latter encouraged a customer to buy what were usually watered-down drinks for her and the patron. The bartender would give the woman a percentage of the cost of the drinks, usually 25 percent. Respectable women who enjoyed an occasional drink were allowed to enter a saloon through the "family entrance" where they could take away their beer in a bucket and their whiskey in a bottle. By 1908 however, licenses were being revoked to saloons allowing gambling and service to women. Also, that year, a federal judge ordered that "dance halls and bawdy saloons" be closed.

Alaska became a US Territory in 1912, and in 1913 women received the right to vote. Soon after, some of the more established Alaska communities began voting to prohibit the sale of alcohol. The evils of alcohol and the saloon atmosphere were being written about in Alaska newspapers, and many lawmakers believed that most, if not all, of Alaska's woes could be traced to people trying to obtain alcohol or acting under its influence. Led by the Women's Christian Temperance Union of Alaska, and Governor John F.A. Strong, the Territorial Legislature voted to once again ban all alcohol. Congressional Delegate (and former Judge) James Wickersham wrote the Alaska "Bone Dry" law which took effect

January 1, 1918. This was a whole two years before the eighteenth amendment to the US Constitution was ratified and the entire nation became dry. The "bone dry" law was exactly as it sounded: it prohibited the manufacture and sale of any and all alcohol. This was so extreme that physicians complained that many people died of influenza because they were not allowed to prescribe medicine containing alcohol.

Second Prohibition: 1918 – 1933

"LAST DAYS OF FRONTIER PASS AWAY" the *Juneau Alaska Daily Empire* reported on January 1, 1918. Describing the party in Juneau the night before, "Several of the bars in the city were completely out of liquor or 'suds' early in the afternoon, but the Alaskan, Gastineau, Grotto, Tucks Place, Montana, Circle City, and New York Exchange had plenty to supply the demand and until the last minute were dishing it out over the bar to the belated revelers. Promptly at the stroke of twelve the patrons of all these places were turned out into the street and the key turned in the locks for the last time."

Alaskans, however, were never really without alcohol. The location of Alaska, the lack of funding for effective law enforcement, and a general apathy toward prohibition by many Alaskans, created a situation where bootlegging and moonshining were extremely lucrative. The proximity of the Southeastern towns to Canada (which had no prohibition) allowed fleets of fishing boats to smuggle in thousands of gallons of 'liquid sunshine'. Stills were set up all over the Alaska Panhandle, and certain towns in other areas were known hotbeds of moonshining: McCarthy, Anchorage, Wasilla, Chickaloon, Nenana, Fairbanks, Tanana, and of course, Nome.

Speakeasies were also common in many towns. These places would operate under the guise of 'soft drink' parlors, pool halls, and cigar stores. Anchorage, with a population of about 1,900, supported thirty to forty establishments where liquor was served. Boats would deliver their cargo to Bootleggers Cove from where it was transported to the speakeasies. Booze was moved from one place to another via a system of underground tunnels – away from the eyes of the territorial police.

End of the 'Bone-Dry' Law: 1933

TERRITORIAL GOVERNOR GEORGE A. PARKS signed the bill repealing the bone-dry law which took effect April 7, 1933. A sense of jubilation rippled through the territory. An editorial in the *Anchorage Daily Times* compared the end of prohibition as "equivalent almost to the delivery of the children of Israel out of the wilderness where for years they wandered famished and athirst." At first, only beer and wine were allowed but neither was readily available. Beer arrived in Juneau on Friday, May 5, 1933. It would be weeks later until deliveries occurred in places like Fairbanks and Nome.

Alaskans were elated when prohibition ended. Harry Race received Beer License No. 1 for his retail store on May 3, 1933. From The Daily Alaska Empire *– May 4, 1933*

Licenses under the new law ranged from $25 for a retail store to $175 for a beverage dispensary license. License No. 40 was issued to Joseph J. Stocker May 16, 1933, for his dispensary, "The Imperial" in Juneau. The Imperial is probably the oldest bar in continuous operation in Alaska.

Dispensaries to Cocktail Bars: 1934 – 1940

ALL LIQUOR BECAME LEGAL IN Alaska on May 1, 1934. However, Alaskans would have to wait until July 1, 1939, when the law allowed them to drink liquor inside a bar. All communities had to vote whether to allow the local dispensaries to serve hard alcohol or not. Dispensaries that did became known as "cocktail bars." The cost of a cocktail license went for five hundred to one thousand dollars, depending on the population of the town. A condition of the law was that no female could tend bar unless her name was on the license; this was finally repealed in 1971. It was after the advent of cocktail bars that the "percentage girls" reappeared, but now they were known as "Bar Girls" or "B-Girls." B-Girls were allowed to encourage customers to buy drinks at Alaska bars, usually at inflated prices, until a measure outlawing the practice was passed in 1959.

WWII and Statehood: 1941 – 1959

WORLD WAR II CHANGED ALASKA more than the gold rushes or the future construction of the trans-Alaska pipeline. The potential for war in the Pacific was a huge concern for the United States in the late 1930s. Military build-up in the form of air bases, ship harbors, and fortifications were constructed all over the territory. A highway connecting Alaska to the Lower 48 states was punched through the Canadian wilderness in 1942. The increasing number of people residing in Alaska provided fuel to the talk of statehood. It also increased the number of bars, particularly in towns like Anchorage and Fairbanks.

In 1951, Anchorage had thirty-two bars and twenty-one liquor stores and a population of 39,242. In 1954, a staggering 3,132,586 gallons of liquor were shipped into Alaska. More than 2.5 million gallons of the total was beer, but almost half a million gallons were classed as hard liquor. This amounted to 17 gallons of intoxicating beverages for every man, woman, child, and infant living in the territory. Alaska became a state on January 3, 1959, and the first Alaska State Legislature created a three-member Alcoholic Beverage Control Board appointed by the Governor.

Oil, areas of prohibition, and tourism: 1960 – present day.

THE DISCOVERY OF A VAST oil field on the North Slope of Alaska in 1968 prompted another rush of people to the state, lured north by the promise of high-paying jobs. The construction of the trans-Alaska oil pipeline prompted many new bars to open in Anchorage and Fairbanks. The economic boom for Alaskans lasted until 1986 when oil prices crashed. However, this increased prosperity highlighted the continuing problem of alcohol and Alaska Natives. In 1979, the State Legislature allowed communities to prohibit the sale and importation of alcoholic beverages. In 1986, the laws were amended to allow communities to prohibit possession of alcohol, and in 1995, Barrow became the largest city in Alaska to ban possession of alcoholic beverages. Barrow has since voted itself "damp" which allows the importation of alcohol for personal consumption.

Since the early 1970s, the tourism industry has transformed towns that could no longer depend on fishing, logging, or the military for a steady income. The cruise ship industry now brings thousands of people to coastal towns, where they are more than willing to purchase clothes, souvenirs, and a drink at a real Alaskan bar.

With the increased national interest in Alaska, the next chapter of Alaska's history with alcohol and its impacts on the population and economy is still being written. The glut of reality television shows that are set in Alaska has highlighted not only the uniqueness of the state, but the undeniable role that bars play in the culture of Alaska.

"GESUNDHEIT—"
"SKAAL"

and

"HERE'S MUD IN YOUR EYE"

Ketchikan's Newest

BEER PARLOR

Opens
TOMORROW
NIGHT
at 8 o'Clock

YOU BUY ONE and
THE HOUSE BUYS ONE

MRS. J. BARSETH
Proprietor

The Fo'c's'le

Opposite American Meat Co.

*From the Ketchikan Alaska Chronicle – June 8, 1934.
312 Front Street (1934 – 2003).*

NOTORIOUS BARS OF SOUTHEAST ALASKA

Southeast Alaska

Arctic Bar
509 Water Street, Ketchikan
(907) 225-4709

License Issued: 1937 to Martin "Mart" Hanson
Amenities: Pool table, darts, TV, liquor store
Find them Online: Facebook

History and Notoriety: The Arctic Bar was located near the Stedman Street Bridge until December 10, 1962, when a record rainfall (7.28" in 24 hours) and subsequent flooding caused Ketchikan Creek to crash into the pilings underneath the two-story building. The bar fell and spilled its entire contents, including cases of liquor, beer, and the safe, into the creek where they floated downstream towards the Tongass Narrows. The 6,200-pound safe was later recovered by a diver in Thomas Basin. The bar moved to its present location in 1963.

In 1947, Mart Hanson sold the original Arctic Bar to Josephine Hill, a prominent Ketchikan businesswoman, who later owned the Potlatch Bar. Ms. Hill was also an "entertainer" and reputedly ran at least one brothel in town as well as several hotels.

The building that currently houses the Arctic Bar was built by the U.S. Forest Service in 1913 and was known as "Dock 13." Over the years, various businesses occupied the building including Ketchikan Air Service and Alaska Coastal Airlines.

Alaskan artist Rie Munoz painted a lithograph of the Arctic Bar in 1980. The captains from the TV show *Deadliest Catch* had a few drinks here in 2007. TV Chef John Pisto filmed 5 shows inside the bar. 3-MAN, a local punk band, recorded *The Arctic Bar Song* in 2018.

☛**Visiting the Arctic Bar:** If you arrive in Ketchikan by cruise ship, the Arctic Bar might be the first business you encounter. Its location at the top of a ramp that leads to the cruise ships is undoubtedly great for business. And Paula Weiss, the very congenial owner and hostess, is more than happy to welcome you to the "Home of the Happy Bears." The deck is a great place to hang out and watch the tourists. There are lots of souvenirs for sale, most of them with the bears doing their happy thing.

Sourdough Bar
(a.k.a. Shipwreck Bar)
301 Front Street, Ketchikan
(907) 225-2217

License Issued: 1950 to George Gouroff
Amenities: Pool tables, dart boards, shuffleboard, liquor store
Find them Online: https://sourdough-bar.edan.io/

History and Notoriety: Harold's Cocktail Bar at 216 Front Street, owned by Harold and Gladys Blanton, was bought by George and Edith Gouroff in 1950, who changed the name to the Sourdough Bar. They owned it for less than a year before selling to Walter "Wally" Kubley and Gordon "Pete" Wilson, who took it over on April 2, 1951. The Kubley family has been in Ketchikan since 1903; Lawrence Kubley, father of Wally, got a dispensary license in May of 1933 and served beer out of the family store. In 1953, when Wally realized how expensive renovating the old building would be, he moved the Sourdough to its current location near the dock. Wally and Pete didn't stay partners for long and when Wally became involved in state politics, he sold the bar to Carroll Bass in 1967. But in 1983, Wally' son Larry bought the bar, and under his management, the Sourdough became the bar it is today, known to many as "the shipwreck bar." Larry passed away in 2021, and Larry's son Wally is the current owner.

Ketchikan had cable television in 1953, which makes it the first city in Alaska to have such a service. According to Donna Luther, a long-time bartender at the Sourdough, the bar was the first business in town to have cable television.

Since 1980, the Sourdough has been known for its unique photo gallery of fishing vessels, ferries, cruise ships, and U.S. Coast Guard Cutters, most of them in some sort of distress. A sign proclaims, "Alaska's Premier Gallery of Maritime Mishaps and Memories." If a boat runs aground near Ketchikan, you can bet a photo of it will eventually appear on the wall of the Sourdough.

☛**Visiting the Sourdough**: The bar is located near the docks and is quite popular with the cruise ship crowd; the Sourdough is often the last stop cruisers make before getting back on board. In addition to the shipwreck photos, there is a collection of U.S. Presidential campaign buttons, trophy sport fish, and a sign on the wall with just the date "January 15, 1920" on it. This is the day prohibition began in the Lower 48 states, 2 whole years after Alaska went "bone dry." The Sourdough loves to celebrate Independence Day.

Totem Bar
314 Front Street, Ketchikan
(907) 225-9521

License Issued: 1941 to Lyman S. and Sibyl T. Ferris
Amenities: Pool table, TV, liquor store
Find them Online: Facebook

History and Notoriety: The Stedman Hotel was built in 1905 and advertised as "Alaska's first luxury hotel." Lyman "Steve" Ferris was born in Canada and was in charge of housing for the Treadwell

Company in Douglas. He bought the Stedman in 1920 and got a beer and wine license for the hotel in May of 1933. In 1937 (when he was 59 years old) he married Sybil (31 years old) who was born in Washington State. The couple opened the Totem Room in January of 1942 on the first floor of the hotel and advertised it as "the most beautiful bar in the northwest." The Stedman was the nicest hotel in town back then, and the Totem Room advertised nightly dancing. Victor Klose and Robert Kline bought the Totem in 1970. In 1979, Klose changed the name to the Totem Bar and moved it from the Stedman to 309 Dock Street. The following year, it moved to 311 Dock Street, and to its current location in 1982.

"Vic" Klose was born in 1927 in Ketchikan to a German father and a Tlingit mother. He served in the Navy during WWII and was a fisherman most of his life. When I met Vic in 2008, he was slim, spry, and seemed happy moving multiple cases of beer from a truck to the bar cooler. He had a poodle named "Muffin" who would come in the front door, jump onto a bar stool, and place her paws on the bar, ready to order a drink. Klose owned the Totem for 54 years and passed away in 2024

John Wayne, the famous actor of western movies, toured the panhandle towns during the 1960s and '70s in his yacht the "Wild Goose" and is said to have frequented the Totem.

The Totem survived the fate of other Ketchikan bars such as the Foc's'le, Alaska, and Pioneer, which were bought out by jewelry franchises. In fact, many framed pictures on the walls of the Totem, and some of the tables, came from these notorious bars.

> ☛**Visiting the Totem:** Some cruise ships will tell their passengers to avoid the Totem, but the tourists love the local flavor. It is known by some as the "native bar" in town, but the bartenders are known to accommodate the cruise ship crowd and whip up the occasional "foo-foo" cocktail. There are many bawdy souvenirs for sale, which match the character of the place.

*Interior of the Totem Room in 1950.
Photo from* Alaska Almanac *by William Tewkesbury.*

Potlatch Bar
126 Thomas Street, Ketchikan
(907) 225-4855

License Issued: 1953 to Carl A. "Tuck" Zaruba and Adelina "Toni" Dickey
Amenities: Pool table, TV's, occasional live music
Find them Online: Facebook

History and Notoriety: The early days of the Potlatch were troubled. Partly because of its location next to the docks, but also due to poor management, the Potlatch was often cited for failing to keep order (keeping drunks out of the bar). Their 1955 attempt to secure an additional retail license was denied because of police reports of incidents at or near the bar. Carl "Tuck" Zaruba lost the bar after less than a year but got it back again in 1956. He sold it to Robert Roberts and Josephine Hill in 1960. "Jo" Hill was a pioneer Ketchikan businesswoman who also owned the Arctic Bar. Born in Ohio in 1894, she began her career in Ketchikan as an "entertainer" and later managed several hotels and possibly brothels. In 1962, Roberts committed suicide in the Potlatch and reportedly haunts the bar to this day. Jo owned the bar until her death in 1970. The story goes that she left the Potlatch to her illegitimate son, who had been raised by the family of an Alaskan Senator. The son, in turn, sold it to Chuck Bellon, a former police officer and commercial fisherman. Leo Norton bought the Potlatch in 1988.

The famous Alaska artist, Rie Munoz, made a beautiful painting of the Potlatch bar in 1984. She offered to sell the original to Chuck Bellon for $150, but he wasn't interested.

Another famous Alaska artist, Ray Troll, said of the Potlatch: "One of the local hangouts I like is the Potlatch Bar in Thomas Basin—the quintessential fisherman's bar right near the docks. It's right out of a Steinbeck novel, and there's great live music there from time to time."

☛**Visiting the Potlatch**: This bar is located close to Creek Street and its throngs of tourists, but it tends to be more of a hangout for locals. Their logo is of the *Jose Maria* and there is a beautiful stained-glass image of the boat at the end of the bar. There is also a chalkboard that displays messages and classifieds. The Potlatch loves to celebrate Independence Day, Halloween, and Christmas.

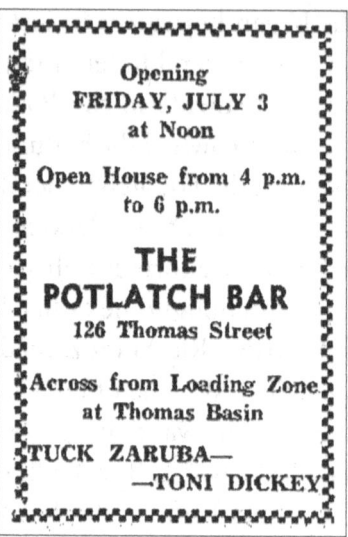

*Opening day at The Potlatch.
From the* Ketchikan Daily News *– July 3, 1953*

49'er Bar
1010 Water Street, Ketchikan
(907) 247-4949

License Issued: 1959 to Frank and Virginia Steiner
Amenities: Pool tables, dart boards, TVs, liquor store
Find them Online: Facebook

History and Notoriety: The 49'er opened the first year of Alaska statehood and its name commemorates the 49th state. The bar was originally located at 1448 Tongass Avenue, moving a few doors down to 1426 Tongass Avenue in 1965. In the early 1970s, the bar doubled as a steak house. It moved to 1008 Water Street in 1992 and then to its current location in 1995.

The building the bar currently occupies was constructed in the 1920s and was used to house a printing company and later the Salvation

Army. The painting of the mermaid with the red slipper used to hang in the old Frontier Saloon. The beautiful bar, wood floors, and the hunting/fishing motif are carefully maintained by owner Steve Turner.

In 2005, the 49'er was where local resident Earl Pickering came after shooting and killing his wife, Carolyn. Mr. Pickering had just been released from prison that morning, after serving 30 days for assaulting Carolyn in the 49'er two months earlier. Mr. Pickering, whose face and clothes were spattered with blood, apparently thought no one would notice. The joke in the bar when someone gets angry is "don't pull a Pickering on me!"

> **Visiting the 49'er:** The pool tables and dart boards are top notch here. Independence Day and New Years Eve are the biggest parties of the year at the 49'er.

Hole in the Wall
7500 (Mile 7.5) South Tongass Way, Ketchikan
(907) 247-2296

License Issued: October 12, 1993, to Marjorie Jackson
Amenities: Pool table, ping pong, food, occasional live music
Find them Online: Facebook

History and Notoriety: Marjorie Jackson, born in Oklahoma, studied recreation and physical therapy in school. She served in the Marine Corps during World War II, and taught soldiers how to swim. In 1966, she moved her son and daughter to Ketchikan and purchased a marina inside a small harbor known as the Hole in the Wall, located seven miles south of town. She was encouraged by friends and her son John ("J.J.") to open a neighborhood bar. She converted an existing boat shed overlooking the marina into the Hole in the Wall.

Marjorie passed away in 2005, and the bar is now owned by her daughter Gail. The bar is frequented by fishermen, sportsmen, and curious tourists. The bar loves to celebrate the Summer Solstice. One year, there were so many people standing on the dock that it sank.

☛**Visiting the Hole in the Wall:** This small bar is in a beautiful location and can be accessed by either car or boat. Finding it by car can be tricky as there is just a hand-painted sign on a tree just off the road. The bar is only open May – September.

Marjorie Jackson (1918 – 2005).
Photo courtesy of Gail Jackson

Hill Bar
(a.k.a. The Hill)
503 Front Street, Craig
(907) 826-3423

License Name Change Issued: September 22, 1978, to Marjorie V. and Alvin C. Young
Amenities: Pool tables, TVs, food, occasional live music, liquor store
Find them Online: Facebook

History and Notoriety: The Hill Bar has its roots in the original Craig Bar that was operated by sisters Elizabeth "Lib" Wahl and Jessie Thompson beginning in 1936. The Craig Bar was also known as "Lib's & Jessie's Cocktail Bar" during the 1940s. Lib passed away in 1960, and Jessie' daughter Marjorie became co-owner in 1963. The colorful Jessie passed away two years later. Marjorie moved the Craig Bar to a location overlooking the water in 1977 and renamed it the Hill Bar in 1978.

Duke Kilbury tells a story in the book *I Never Did Mind the Rain* that he moved to Craig in 1936 and became acquainted with Jessie and her husband Leslie V. "Tommy" Thompson who owned the bakery in town. One night after playing cards, the Thompson' invited Duke back to their living quarters adjacent to the bar. They said, "We're going south and we want you to take care of the bar for us." Even though Duke was a newcomer to Craig, the Thompson' turned the bar over to him, leaving in November and not returning until March.

Michael McGuire, in his book *Angels to Ashes* describes the three bars in Craig during the early 1980s. Regarding the Hill Bar "fishermen and loggers and Alaska road crews gathered at the Hill Bar; known to locals as 'The Hill.' A little strange, a little dingy, a wall of windows that had a view of the public float and just two blocks from downtown. The Hill also was the roughest bar in Craig. On weekends it was nothing to have a large brawl breakout, (sic) usually loggers, against road crews, against fisherman." McGuire also reports that John Kenneth Peel, the only person ever tried for the unsolved murder of eight people that were aboard the fishing boat *Investor* in 1982, was first located by State Troopers having a beer at the Hill Bar.

Marjorie Young, daughter of Jessie Thompson, died in 2020. Her son, Ralph Mackie, is the current owner.

☛**Visiting the Hill Bar:** The Hill Bar is indeed on a small hill just off the main drag in Craig. The dance floor is large and a big draw on the weekends. Checking out the graffiti in the men's room reveals that the rivalry between loggers and fishermen is alive and well in Craig.

Craig Inn
403 Water Street, Craig
(907) 826-3365

License Issued: 1947 to Edward R. Otto and Anna M. Dye
Amenities: Pool table, food, liquor store
Find them Online: Facebook (T.K.'s Café)

History and Notoriety: Edward R. "Joe" Otto was born in Washington state in 1892. Anna M. Scott, born in Wisconsin in 1896, married Charles P. Dye in Portland, Oregon in 1922. Two years later, their son Charles Jr. was born, and then tragically, Charles Sr. died. In 1935, Anna and Charles Jr. moved to Craig where she partnered with Otto to open a restaurant, which they named the Craig Inn. In 1936, the inn got a beer and wine license. Huge pink salmon runs during the 1930s contributed to the growth of Craig. In 1947, Otto and Dye bought the liquor license for Gil's Bar in Craig from owner Gilmore Reese.

In 1950, the citizens of Craig voted their community dry. The vote was close: 90 to 87. Otto and Dye, along with Jessie Thompson from the Craig Bar, spearheaded a successful effort to void the vote. The Craig Inn and Gil's Bar operated separately until Otto left Alaska in 1957. By then the Craig Inn consisted of a bar, liquor store, hotel, and restaurant. 1957 was also the year the Craig cannery burned down.

In 1959, Dye sold the Craig Inn to Edrie and Evelyn Thomas, who were living in Ketchikan. Five years later, the couple advertised that the Craig Inn was for sale, adding that it was a "Good business" and "Owner wishes to retire." They finally sold the bar to their son Donald Thomas and his wife Karen in 1971. Donald' brother Robert and his wife Diane became partners in the business in 1973. In 1977, the Craig Inn moved to its current location on Water Street. Later that year, Donald Thomas passed away. The Thomas family sold the bar to John B. McKinley in 1980.

Michael McGuire, in his book *Angels to Ashes* describes the three bars in Craig during the early 1980s. Compared to the Hill Bar "The Craig Inn is more subdued, far less rowdy but rougher around the edges. The Craig Inn has very few windows, natural light was nonexistent, and the bar was long and behind it stood a wall of dusty booze bottles. The floor was well worn wood; years of loggers with cork boots had left their mark. A clientele of ex-cons, drug dealers, and other not so clean individuals mingle with the locals."

John McKinley was born in Ketchikan in 1946 and grew up there. In the 1970s he worked as a truck driver on the Alaska Pipeline. He owned the Craig Inn for forty years before passing away in Mexico in 2020. His daughter Chanel is now the owner.

Visiting the Craig Inn: There is no mistaking the Craig Inn. The hot pink (magenta) color building is easy to find. Inside, TK's Café serves hot sandwiches to have with your libations. The bar is popular with fisherman, loggers, and tourists alike.

From The Alaska Fisherman's Almanac for 1947. *Edited by Ballard Hadman*

Glacier Inn
International Street, Hyder
(250) 636-9248

License Issued: 1950 to Mary Meger
Amenities: Pool table, food, liquor store.

History and Notoriety: Paul and Mary "Marie" Meger came to Hyder in 1920. Paul, from Illinois, and Marie, from New York, were both born in 1888. Paul was a miner, and the 1920s were the mining boom years for Hyder. Paul also ran an illegal watering hole on the American side of the border, and Marie (known affectionately as "Dago" Marie) ran a legal brothel on the Canadian side. They left Hyder for a time but came back in 1950 and opened the Glacier Inn. Because they didn't have a till for the money, the dollar bills ended up in Marie' ample brassiere: big bills went in the right cup ("The Bank of America" as the miners called it) and the small bills went in the left cup ("The Bank of Montreal").

Over the course of 70 years, dollar bills have been attached to the walls of the Glacier Inn. Early miners started the tradition, signing the bills to ensure they had enough for a drink if they came to town broke. Today, there are thousands of dollar bills, with denominations from countries worldwide.

Marie and Paul retired in 1957 and moved to Portland, Oregon, where Paul passed away in 1959 and Marie in 1974. Lloyd Fillion owned the Glacier Inn until 1978, when he sold it to Marie and James Bunn.

The movie *Leaving Normal* (1992) starring Christine Lahti and Meg Tilly was shot partially in Hyder. The Glacier Inn appears in the movie but is disguised as the "Eternity Bar."

☛**Visiting the Glacier Inn**: The Glacier Inn is *the place* in town to get "Hyderized" which means drinking a shot of Everclear (180 proof grain alcohol). After downing the shot, known as a "Snakebite," the bartender will traditionally touch a match to the shot glass, producing a pretty blue flame. If possible, time your visit to Hyder in early July. Hyder and the neighboring Canadian town of Stewart celebrate "International Days" July 1 – 4, which is the biggest party of the year. Remember to get some Canadian currency, which is preferred by local businesses.

Totem Bar
116 Front Street, Wrangell
(907) 874-3533

License Name Change Issued: 1949 to Eugene J. Wheeler
Amenities: Pool tables, foosball, TVs, liquor store

History and Notoriety: The building that houses the Totem Bar was built in 1908 and was then the Wrangell (later Wheeler)

Drug store. The original bar was across the street and began as a billiard hall, run by L.A. "Ole" Olsen. In the 1940s it was known as Moore's Cocktail Bar, run by Charlie Moore and Eugene Wheeler. Wheeler, who was also a dentist in town, changed the name to the Totem in 1949. He moved the bar across the street after the building burned in the great fire of March 21, 1952. The bar first occupied the space where the liquor store is now.

Fred and Leonard Angerman bought the bar in 1961 and expanded into the rest of the building in 1967. The Angerman brothers, who were both born in Wrangell, tended the bar while their wives "hopped tables." The bar was popular with loggers and fishermen alike.

The Angerman' sold the bar to Perry and Kimberly Brink in 1999. It was while the Brink's owned the Totem that the bar became famous for its "Can-Can Troupe." Six lovely young ladies, wearing gold rush period costumes with garter belts, would entertain the crowd with singing and dancing. Customers could get a meal and see the show two or three times a day during the summer months. The Angerman's bought the Totem back in 2007. Aaron Powell is the current owner.

☞Visiting the Totem: No trip to Wrangell is complete without stopping in at this historic bar. I was lucky and met one of the original can-can girls, some of whom still occasionally visit the bar. Wrangell Tent City Days in February and the 4th of July are prime times to visit the Totem. On July 4th, you are allowed to buy a drink at any bar in Wrangell and take it "to go."

The Angerman Bros at The Totem Bar (Wrangell) sometime during the 1960s. Photo courtesy of Leonard Angerman

---

Rayme's Bar
(a.k.a. The Brig)
532 Front Street, Wrangell
(907) 874-3442

License Issued: June 1955 to Brigham Young Grant and William D. Grant
Amenities: Pool tables, TVs, occasional live music, liquor store
Find them Online: Facebook

History and Notoriety: Rayme's is named for its current owner Rayme Privett, a local man who knew that he wanted to tend bar since he was in the 8th grade. To many folks, this bar will be forever known by its original name "The Brig" after the first owner. According to census records, Brigham Grant was originally from Idaho. He had been the town Postmaster and his son William the assistant Postmaster. The word brig also refers to the fact that rebar once covered all the windows, which made it look you were inside a jail, or had just been "thrown into the brig." In 1986, the bar name changed to The Shady Lady Brig Bar which was used until 2007 when Rayme took over.

The bar had a reputation for being the roughest in town, which might have been one of the reasons it was chosen for a fight scene in the 1973 movie *The Timber Tramps* (a.k.a. *The Big Push*) starring Claude Akins, Joseph Cotton, Cesar Romero, and Rosey Grier. A handwritten sign that appeared at Rayme's on January 1, 2017, stated "All Parties Involved With Fighting inside This Bar Will Be Thrown Out For 30 days. This Includes Pushing and Shoving."

☛**Visiting Rayme's:** During the Wrangell Tent City Days celebration in February, Rayme's was the scene of the Shady Lady Ball, which gave folks (men and women) the opportunity to dress like a shady lady. Most guys traditionally wear bowler hats for the ball. Hopefully this event will return. Rayme's usually has live music on weekends, and definitely for occasions on St. Patrick's Day and Independence Day.

```
         Grand        Opening       Tonight  !
                       THE   BRIG
Open  House  9  to  10  p. m.     Dancing 'til  Midnight     Live  Music
   B. Y. Grant                      Phone  253                 W. D. Grant
```

Grand opening of The Brig. From The Wrangell Sentinel *– August 19, 1955.*

Marine Bar
640 Shakes Street, Wrangell
(907) 874-3005

License Issued: May 1953 to Virgil Neyman
Amenities: Pool table, darts, TVs, food, liquor store
Find them Online: Facebook (Hungry Beaver Pizza and Marine Bar)

History and Notoriety: The Harbor Café became the Marine Bar in May of 1953. The bar was owned by Alan and Margaret McCoy during the 1960s and '70s, burning down twice during that time. The original bar could only seat nine customers, so each time it was rebuilt it was also expanded. It was under the ownership of Patty Kautz, beginning in 1982 that the Marine Bar took on its current character.

The ceiling of the Marine is the most defining characteristic of this bar. Patty came up with the idea of "selling" the large ceiling tiles to local businesses and charter boats to advertise, and for regular customers to express themselves. Several of the tiles are memorials to loved ones who have passed on. Local artist "Kitty" Angerman can take credit for many of the most beautiful tiles, which look like oil paintings. Alaskan artist Ray Troll lent his talent to one of the tiles in 1997.

☛**Visiting the Marine Bar:** The pizza is a big incentive to come to the Marine. The dough is made from a special recipe, and a hot slice tastes awesome with a cold beer. The Marine is very popular during the Wrangell Tent City Days in February. The bar also does some special send-off parties for the local commercial fishermen in May and September.

```
┌─────────────────────────────┐
│        NOW OPEN             │
│      MARINE BAR             │
│      (FORMER HARBOR CAFE)   │
│         Cocktails           │
│       Beer  ·  Wine         │
│   FIRST STOP and LAST CHANCE│
│         PHONE 144           │
└─────────────────────────────┘
```

First ad. The Wrangell Sentinel – *May 22, 1953.*

Harbor Bar (Petersburg)

310 North Nordic Drive, Petersburg
(907) 772-4526

License Issued: May 24, 1946, to Fred R. Porter and Leon Simpson
Amenities: Pool table, shuffleboard, TVs, occasional live music, liquor store
Find Them Online: Facebook

History and Notoriety: The history of the Harbor Bar began with Julius Sunde, who ran a card room and pool hall near this location in 1913. Charlie Mann took over the pool hall in 1920 and began selling beer to his customers in 1933. Willie Johnson bought the bar in 1939, and then sold it to Ernie Carter in 1943, the same Ernie Carter who owned Ernie's Cocktail Bar in Sitka. Both bars shared the name Ernie's Cocktail Bar. Carter sold the bar in Petersburg to Fred Porter and Leon Simpson in May of 1946, and the name changed to the Harbor Bar. Porter was born in Oregon in 1886, had been a fireman, and had a wife and daughter that were both named Hannah. An old sign in the bar from the Fred Porter days reads "Porters Hannah Liquor Store." Porter sold the bar to N.A. MacEachran in 1947, who then sold it to Frederick "Ted" and Violet Reynolds in 1948. Ted was born in 1907 in Washington state and came to Alaska in 1928. During WWII, he served in the US Army and was stationed in the Aleutian Islands. The building was damaged by fires in 1951 and 1959. Ted Reynolds died in 1966, and in 1969, the building housing the bar was torn down. That same year, a new building named after Ted Reynolds on Main Street (now Nordic Drive), became the home of the Harbor Bar. Morris Mattson owned the bar from 1973 to 1986, and sold it to Larry and Shirley Matheny, who owned it through the 1990s. Darcy Caples and Curt Birchell are the current owners.

The Harbor Bar, like many businesses in Petersburg, reflects the Nordic heritage of its citizens, which includes bathrooms for Vikings and Valkyries. A huge 50-pound red snapper caught in 1980 hangs on the wall as does a poster advertising the 1974 concert at the bar by famous country singer Tex Williams, who undoubtedly sang his hit song *Smoke, smoke, smoke that cigarette!* The bar sponsors a local women's softball team, the "Eager Beavers."

☞**Visiting the Harbor Bar:** The bar has a long list of specialty cocktails, but don't count on them using a blender for any of them. Cannery pay days are popular here, as is St. Patrick's Day, Independence Day, Halloween (costume contest) and the Little Norway Festival held in May every year.

Harbor Bar
Formerly Ernie's Cocktail Bar
COME IN -- BRING YOUR FRIENDS
and ENJOY OUR HOSPITALITY
WE AIM TO PLEASE

First ad. Petersburg Press – June 14, 1946.

Kito's Kave
200 Chief John Lott Street, Petersburg
(907) 772-3207

License Issued: June 1, 1965, to Richard Kito
Amenities: Pool tables, foosball, TVs, occasional live music, liquor store
Find them Online: Facebook (kitos.kave)

History and Notoriety: Kito's Kave can trace its roots back to the Dory Bar, which opened in 1910 in the old Hadland building. The Dory became a café during prohibition, a bar again in 1934 known as OK's Place, then the Petersburg Bar in 1944. Richard "Dick" Kito bought the bar in 1965, renamed it Kito's Kave, and then moved it to its current location in 1972. The building it occupies was once Sing Lee's General Store.

Kito (1931 – 1987) was a life-long resident and prominent Petersburg businessman, who was very active in local and state affairs, state commander of the American Legion, and city mayor four times. He died of cancer at the young age of 56 and is buried in the Petersburg Memorial Cemetery.

"Every town has a Harbor Bar, but there's only one Kito's Kave" says James "Jimmie" Swanson, a co-owner of the bar. The bar does have a reputation for being occasionally rowdy. During the annual Little Norway festival, folks dressed up as Vikings crowd the bar. Some of these Vikings will have real swords and axes with them. You can see the evidence (nicks and gouges) on some of the wooden tables.

> **Visiting Kito's Kave:** The large dance floor and regular DJ make Kito's the place to be, especially on the weekends. Super Bowl weekend, Fat Tuesday, the Little Norway

Festival, Independence Day, Halloween (costume contest) are popular times to visit Kito's Kave.

First ad. Petersburg Press – July 2, 1965.

Richard Kito. Petersburg Press – October 8, 1969.

Ernie's Bar
(a.k.a. Ernie's Old Time Saloon)
130 Lincoln Street, Sitka
(907) 747-3334

License Issued: September 27, 1941, to Ernest L. Carter
Amenities: Pool tables, darts, TVs, occasional live music
Find them Online: Facebook

History and Notoriety: "Ernie" Carter, born in Washington state in 1901, had been a bartender in Juneau and in Sitka before opening his own bar. The *Sitka Sentinel* reported that a large crowd showed up for opening night on a rainy Thursday, October 16, 1941, and that the bar "is made for rapid service and mixing ability." Two years later, Ernie opened a second bar (also called Ernie's) in Petersburg, which became the Harbor Bar in 1946. The Navy established an Air Station in Sitka in 1939, and in 1941 the Army established Fort Ray and Fort Rousseau. Between the military, the fisherman, and the pulp mill workers (1959 – 1993) Ernie's enjoyed a steady clientele.

Ernie and his wife Jean divorced in 1950, and Jean was awarded ownership of the bar. Ernie moved to Sweet Home, Oregon, opened a bar/restaurant, and passed away in 1961. Jean left Sitka in 1957 but owned the bar until 1965. That same year, Stan Filler became a partner in the bar, and then owner in 1978. He became interested in city and state politics, and served as Mayor of Sitka in the late 1990s.

The bar was known first as Ernie's Cocktail Bar, but by the 1960s was known simply as Ernie's. The "Old Time Saloon" descriptor dates from the mid-1980s. Bowling and basketball teams sponsored by Ernie's are known as the "Old Timers." Since the closing of the Columbia Bar in 2011, Ernie's is the oldest bar in Sitka.

☛**Visiting Ernie's Bar:** The bar is not large, and can be crowded at times, but this lends to the charm of the place. Note the "Side Hill Salmon" mounted on the wall. Music can be found here on the weekends. St. Patrick's Day, Independence Day, and Alaska Days (mid-October) are popular times to visit Ernie's.

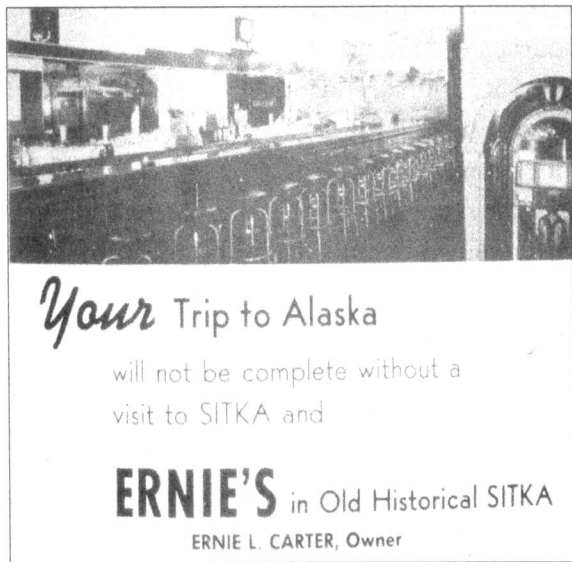

From Lou Jacobin's Guide to Alaska – 1946.

Pioneer Bar
(a.k.a. P-Bar)
212 Katlian Street, Sitka
(907) 747-3456

License Issued: December 1951 to Roy Herrin and Harry Thorburn
Amenities: Pool tables, darts, TVs, food, liquor store.
Find them Online: Facebook

History and Notoriety: On January 3, 1952, Roy Herrin and Harry Thorburn announced in the *Daily Sitka Sentinel* that they had purchased Howard Bradshaw's bar, known as "Brad's Place" and the adjoining liquor store and changed the name to the Pioneer Bar and Liquor Store. Both Herrin and Thorburn and their families were living in Wrangell when they bought the bar. The "P-Bar" has been serving a steady clientele of fisherman, serviceman, loggers, and tourists ever since. Adolf Thomsen and Robert Wyman took over in 1956, and Harold Sulzer owned it from 1963 to 1987. The bar was originally located at 312 Katlian Street but moved to its present location in 1960.

In 1962, a safe from the bar containing several thousand dollars was stolen and later recovered, without the cash of course. In 1966, two men robbed the bar of $2,500 in cash and took a cab to the airport, where they had a chartered a flight to take them to Juneau. After the plane was enroute, the bandits hijacked it to Ketchikan. The "flying bandits" were arrested two weeks later.

In 2015, the name of an annual event held at the Pioneer known as the "slave auction" was changed to "Alaska Day Auction." This was in response to a complaint from the Anchorage Chapter of the NAACP. The auction, where people donate two hours of their time to perform chores, has been a part of the Alaska Day celebration (October 18) for many years. All proceeds go to charities.

In recent years, the Great Guinness Toast in February has become a big event at the P-Bar. Members of the all-male Seattle Firefighters "Pipes and Drums" band entertain the crowds with Irish favorites, all decked out in kilts and berets.

☛Visiting the Pioneer Bar: The bar is equipped with comfortable booths, which fill up fast on weekend nights. The walls are covered with framed photos of a wide variety of fishing vessels The Great Guinness Toast in February, St. Patrick's Day, Independence Day, and Halloween (costume contest) are popular times to visit the P-Bar.

> BE YE LANDLUBBER OR TAR,
>   YE'RE WELCOME AT THE PIONEER BAR.
> DISCUSS WEATHER OR WAR
>   DOWN AT THE PIONEER BAR.
> IF YOU DRINK FROM GLASS OR JAR,
>   WE'LL FILL 'ER UP AT THE PIONEER BAR.
> YOU'LL FIND THE DOOR AJAR
>   DOWN AT THE PIONEER BAR.
> WE WELCOME PEASANT OR CZAR
>   DOWN AT THE PIONEER BAR.
> FISHERMEN ARE NEVER A LIAR
>   WITH THEIR TALES AT PIONEER BAR.
> HITCH YOUR WAGON TO A STAR,
>   HITCH YOUR CHAIR TO THE PIONEER BAR.
> GET YOUR ROSE ATTAR
>   AT THE PIONEER BAR.
> COME HITHER, COME HERE, COME H'YAR
>   TO THE PIONEER BAR.
> BY FOOT, SLED OR CAR,
>   COME TO THE PIONEER BAR.
> YOU MAY COME FROM NEAR OR AFAR,
>   BUT YOU'RE WELCOME AT THE PIONEER BAR.
> CATCH SALMON, HALIBUT, OR GAR,
>   LEARN HOW AT THE PIONEER BAR.
>   C. U.

From the Daily Sitka Sentinel – *May 14, 1968.*

Rose's Bar & Grill
112 Salmon Way, Pelican
(907) 735-2288

License Issued: November 2, 1973, to Rose Perley
Amenities: TV, food
Find them Online: Facebook

History and Notoriety: Miland Soule and his wife Dollie opened the Lisianski Bar (a.k.a. Soule's Bar) at this location in 1939. After Rose (Perley) Miller took over, the bar became world famous and is truly one of the most notorious bars in Alaska. Even the Alcoholic Beverage Control (ABC) Board used "notorious" and "rough and rowdy" to describe Rose's.

Rose (pronounced "rosy") was born in 1933 and moved to Pelican in 1971 after her damaged tugboat was towed there. The bar's grand opening in July 1973 attracted many well-wishers including Perry Harris, owner of the Red Dog, and Bob Schroth, owner of the Imperial, two well-established Juneau institutions. Over the years, Rose threw many parties and invited lots of people to "take off their pants" and dance on the bar.

I had the privilege of interviewing Rose in 2008. She told me "My customers are what makes this bar famous. They're the ones running around without their clothes on. They're the ones dancing on the bar. Thousands of people have danced on my bar. If people don't like it, they shouldn't come in here."

She also told me a story about a "hard-core" Christian woman who took her hand and prayed for her, asking forgiveness for all the sins that have occurred in her bar. Then the woman bought two of her t-shirts, with the slogan on back "Take off your pants. Let's have a party." Rose sold her bar at least twice, and both times she bought it back. In 1992, twenty determined fishermen boycotted the bar until Rose returned. Rose retired in 2017 and passed away in 2024. Steve Daniels is the current owner.

I recall the ferry ride back to Juneau from Pelican on Memorial Day in 2008. The Boardwalk Boogie event had just concluded, and I was eavesdropping on a young woman talking on the phone. She was describing the night before which began at Rose's. "If I wondered if I was going to hell before now," she said, "last night sealed the deal."

☛**Visiting Rose's:** The bar has the same floor, ceiling, and piano as the Lisianski Bar. The ceiling is covered with signatures and sentiments from many years of happy customers. Cinco de Mayo (Rose's birthday is May 7), and Independence Day are popular times to be at Rose's.

*Rose at the grand opening of her bar – 1973.
Photo courtesy of the family of Rose Miller*

The Office Bar
(a.k.a Kooteeya Bar)
151 Front Street, Hoonah
(907) 945-3215

License Issued: August 4, 2003, to Mary Erickson
Amenities: Pool table, TVs, food
Find them Online: Facebook

History and Notoriety: The Office Bar can trace its roots back to the Koffee Kup Kafe and Bar that Elizabeth "Liz" Martin opened in 1970 in the center of town. Two years later, Martin moved her establishment down to the beach and renamed it the Down the Beach Bar. James "Jim" Austin Jr. and his wife Irene bought the bar in 1979, and renamed it the Kooteeya, which is the Tlingit word for totem pole. The polished wooden bar reportedly came from The Whaler, a downtown Juneau bar which at one point had used the surface for a shuffleboard. The bar gained a reputation for catering to a rough crowd, which in Alaska usually means loggers and fisherman. The 1980s and '90s were good economic years for both groups.

In 2003, Jim sold the bar to his niece Mary Erickson, and her husband Jim. The couple changed the name of the bar because one of the bartenders, Dottie Johanson, who had worked at the bar since the Koffee Kup days, referred to it as her "office."

Under the Erickson's management, the bar has cleaned up and improved its reputation. So much so that *Esquire* magazine declared The Office as one of the best bars in America for the year 2006. The article refers to the very generous patrons who rang the house bell many times during the authors visit, and "…the realization that bars like this hadn't been seen in southeast Alaska since the cruise ships took over in the eighties."

☛**Visiting The Office:** If you're in Hoonah on a cruise stop or doing the zip rider, don't leave town before stopping in at The Office. Their motto is "Good Times and Friends," and patrons are sure to find both. During the summer months, enjoy the delicious freshly steamed Dungeness crabs.

Red Dog Saloon
278 South Franklin Street, Juneau
(907) 463-3658

License Name Change Issued: 1950 to Earl T. Forsythe and Raymond Mansfield
Amenities: TVs, food, live entertainment
Find them Online: www.reddogsaloon.com; Facebook

History and Notoriety: Earl Forsythe, owner of Baileys Bar, and his partner Ray Mansfield renamed the bar the Red Dog Saloon, opening on December 23, 1950. The location of Bailey's was at 162 South Franklin Street near the Alaskan Hotel, in a building which once housed the Germania Saloon. Forsythe fashioned the Red Dog after a bar he had visited in New York City that had an 1890s look with sawdust on the floor and bartenders in costume. The Red Dog moved across the street to 159 South Franklin in 1966.

The Red Dog has a history of providing entertainment, specifically piano players. Back in 1955, it was "Rag Time Bob" who tickled the ivories with such favorites as "No One Loves Me Like My Tomato Can." Possibly the most famous of the Red Dog piano players was Hattie Jessup, also known as "Ragtime Hattie," "Silver Dollar Hattie" and "Juneau Hattie." The self-described "Queen of Ragtime," Hattie played at the Red Dog every summer in the late 1950s and early 1960s, wearing white gloves and a silver dollar halter top. She had a vast repertoire of songs, and if you asked her to play a song she didn't know, you were given a free drink.

Gordon "Gordie" Kanouse, who bought the Red Dog in 1952, owned a mule and he and the animal would lure tourists into the saloon by wearing a sign that read "Follow my ass to the Red Dog Saloon." Apparently, owning the Red Dog and a mule didn't provide enough fulfillment in life, and Gordie decided to end his own in 1968. His wife Virginia managed the Red Dog until 1972, when she sold it to Donald and Perry Harris. The Harris' moved the bar to its current location in 1988 on a lot that was once occupied by Sweeney's Corner Bar.

Hanging on the wall of the Red Dog, behind the bar, is a pistol that might have been owned by Wyatt Earp, the famous lawman of the 19th century. According to the placard, Earp, on his way back to his home in Nome, checked the pistol in with the local Marshall on June 27, 1900. The ship left for Nome early on June 29 before Wyatt could reclaim the weapon. It was retained by the Marshall and later sold to a private collector. It is a fact that Wyatt and Josie lived in Nome, where they owned the Dexter saloon. However, according to Josie' biography, the couple were in Denver on July 6, 1900, when they learned that Wyatt's brother Warren had been shot to death in Wilcox, AZ. Allowing for inaccuracies in dates, it is possible that the pistol once belonged to Earp.

☛**Visiting the Red Dog Saloon**: The Red Dog Saloon is the most visited bar in all Southeast Alaska. Its proximity to the cruise ship docks means that hundreds of visitors pass through "those swingin' doors." Many Juneauites consider the Red Dog a "tourist bar" and avoid it. However, it does have a certain charm and deserves a visit, especially if you've never had a Duck Fart, a specialty of the house.

Hattie Jessup at the Red Dog Saloon – 1962.
Alaska State Library, P474-56

Lucky Lady Pub
192 South Franklin Street, Juneau
(907) 586-9673

License Name Change Issued: 1970 to Mary Joyce
Amenities: Pool tables, TV's
Find them Online: Facebook

History and Notoriety: In 1946, Mary Joyce bought an interest in a new bar called the Pamaray Club in the Fashion Building on South Franklin Street. Her partners were Eli ("Pa") and Marchetta ("Ma") Ray. Joyce was by this time an Alaskan celebrity of sorts, having made a successful (and highly publicized) thousand-mile solo trek with a dog sled team from Taku Lodge (90 miles by boat northeast of Juneau) to Fairbanks in the winter of 1935.

Joyce was born in Wisconsin in 1899 and came to Alaska in 1929. She owned the Taku Lodge from 1934 – 1942, and even though she was once quoted as saying "Oh, I haven't the least bit of business ability!" she had an interest in not only the Pamaray but also the Top Hat Club, another popular Juneau establishment. Joyce was very sympathetic to the plight of Juneau bachelors, and served huge turkey dinners at both bars every Thanksgiving and Christmas.

Joyce had many interests, all of which involved adventure and people. She was a certified nurse, a pilot, and even an airline stewardess. She also ran unsuccessfully for a seat in the Territorial House in 1950. Though, her interests never included marriage.

By 1963, both Pa and Ma Ray had passed on, and Joyce shared ownership of the bar with Bill Ray, son of Pa and Ma Ray. Ray also became interested in politics and served as a House representative and then the State Senate. Joyce took full ownership of the Pamaray in 1969 and in 1970, moved the bar next door and changed the name to the Lucky Lady, her nickname for herself.. She lived upstairs above the bar until her death in 1976 of a heart attack. In February 2013, Mary Joyce was inducted into the Alaska Women's Hall of Fame.

☛**Visiting the Lucky Lady:** The bar celebrates the life of Joyce through placards and photos. Mary was Irish and proud of it and this bar observes St. Patrick's Day in a big way.

Left to right: famed aviator Joe Crossort, Mary Joyce, and Governor Ernest Gruening. From the article "Mary of the Snows" by Churchill Fisher. Alaska Life magazine – September 1944

Alaskan Hotel Bar
167 South Franklin Street, Juneau
(907) 318-9470

License Issued: 1979 to Mike and Bettye Adams
Amenities: Pool table, occasional live music
Find them Online: www.thealaskanhotel.com; Facebook

History and Notoriety: I am grateful to Joshua Adams, whose book *The Life and Times of the Alaskan Hotel* provided much of what follows. The Alaskan Hotel officially opened for business on September 16, 1913. Omer H. Patton was the first manager of the bar, which was also called the "sample room."

The bar was described as open and spacious and a magnet to the upper crust of Juneau society. When prohibition closed all bars, the Alaskan establishment stayed open by serving soda and ice cream sundaes. Dave Housel, who managed the hotel during those years, was still in charge in 1933 when prohibition ended. However, his application for a beer license was initially denied on the grounds that he was "not a suitable person." The bar began dispensing beer on July 1, 1933.

During the 1950s, the Alaskan Hotel had a resident Madame named "Mary" who rented out rooms to her girls. Many arrangements were made in the bar for services to be rendered in the rooms upstairs. In 1960, Marguerite Franklin took over management of the hotel and changed its name to the Northlander. She leased out the basement to Ace Byrnie, who moved there. The Northlander bar was known by many locals as the Snake Pit, where all manner of humanity such as prostitutes, drug-dealers, swindlers, musicians, and dirty politicians came to drink and rub elbows.

Actor John Wayne stayed at the Northlander once and started drinking at the bar before heading next door to the old Red Dog Saloon. The Duke was said to have paid for each round with a one-hundred-dollar bill, telling the bartenders to keep the change each time. Since he was staying at the hotel, some of the staff went to retrieve him when they heard he was very drunk. They tried to help him up the stairs, but he got away from them (he was a large man, after all) and fell down the entire first flight. The next day, the Duke didn't remember the incident.

Byrnie set up a room on the first floor, especially for gambling. The room is at the back of the present-day bar and is known as the Bird Room. In this room, deeds to several local establishments, including the Red Dog and the Triangle, were reported to have changed hands. It is said that Perry Harris got title to the Red Dog over a card game here. The room today is used today for informal musical jam sessions.

In 1977, the bar was shut down after a police raid and Byrnie lost his liquor license. The fire marshal then shut down the hotel. Franklin sold the Northlander to Laura McCarly, who threw a party that left the bar totally dry and then gave everything back to Franklin when her check bounced! Franklin then sold the hotel to Mike and Bettye Adams, who restored to the hotel, its original name, and renovated the bar, which re-opened on June 5, 1981. The Alaskan Hotel and Bar was added to the National Register of Historic Places on October 25, 1978.

> **Visiting the Alaskan:** The owners have done a great job restoring this classic notorious bar. Several celebrities have stayed at the Alaskan and drank there, including writer Ken Kesey, actor Mel Gibson, activist and politician Ralph Nader, ESPN reporter Michael Wilbon, rock band Red Hot Chili Peppers, and actor Ted Danson, who allegedly drank Jagermeister and tipped the bartender with marijuana buds.
>
> If you are not from Alaska, order an Alaskan beer and introduce yourself to a local. That way you can say "I drank an Alaskan with an Alaskan at the Alaskan."

A gathering of men at the Alaskan Hotel Bar – circa 1917. Photo courtesy of Cheryl Lewis.

Triangle Club
(a.k.a. The Triangle)
251 Front Street, Juneau
(907) 586-3140

License Name Change Issued: 1935 to Wilbur Burford and Emmett Bothello
Amenities: TVs, Pinochle table
Find them Online: https://www.triangleclubbar.com/ ; Facebook

History and Notoriety: The Winter and Pond building, which houses the Triangle Club, was built in 1900 and is one of several buildings on the block that originally sat on pilings. Wilbur Burford and his brother Jack were managing the Burford's Corner bar at this location in 1933.

In 1935, Wilbur Burford and his new partner Emmett Bothello changed the name to the Triangle Inn. By 1939, Burford was the sole owner, and it became known as the Triangle Bar. Burford sold to William Eddy and Joseph J. "Papa Joe" Thomas, Sr. in 1947 and the "grand opening" was on St. Patrick's Day. In 1948, "Papa Joe" became the sole owner, and in 1949 he changed the name to the Triangle Club.

Papa Joe was born in Pennsylvania in 1915, moved to Alaska in 1938 and married Bessie Powers from Juneau. They had three children including Joe Jr., who joined in the operation of the bar in 1966. Papa Joe retired in 1976 and passed away in 1983. Leanne Thomas, daughter of Joe Jr., is the current owner.

Back when Papa Joe ran the bar, there was a barber shop adjacent to the club. Gentleman patrons could come in for a "warm up" before or after getting a cut or a shave. Papa Joe invested in a pinochle table, the only bar in Juneau that has one. Actor John Wayne, on one of his many cruises through Southeast Alaska, stopped in at the Triangle Club and played a few hands.

The Triangle Club is reportedly haunted by the ghost of Thomas Powers. "Uncle Tommy" lived upstairs above the bar for many years. Leanne Thomas told me that the bar was like his living room. Uncle Tommy died in 1997 at the age of seventy-six but has since made his presence known through the usual acts of mischief.

> **Visiting the Triangle Club**: The Thomas family has collected many historical photos of the Juneau area and have placed them on display throughout. The bar is indeed triangular. The pinochle table is still there, with a regularly scheduled game. Celebrating Independence Day at the Triangle Club provides an excellent view of the parade. Halloween and the "end of tourist season" party are noted celebrations. The Triangle Club sponsors a women's soccer team called "The Triangle's."

First ad. The Daily Alaska Empire – *February 23, 1935.*

Imperial Bar
241 Front Street, Juneau
(907) 586-1960

License Issued: May 16, 1933, to Joseph J. Stocker
Amenities: Pool tables, dart boards, TV's, food
Find them Online: https://www.theimperialbar.com/; Facebook

History and Notoriety: The Imperial is reputed to be the latest in the evolution of bars at this location, beginning with the Missouri in 1891 and the Louvre in 1896. However, the Louvre was almost destroyed by fire in 1906. It was rebuilt, but by 1917 it had changed hands and was doing business as Tuck's Place, which closed at the end of the year because of the Alaska "Bone Dry" Law.

Meanwhile, J. Homer and Joseph J. "J.J." Stocker opened the Imperial Billiard Parlor in 1914 inside the Jaeger Building at 201 S. Franklin Street. The Louvre building was used as a department store until Stocker bought it in 1928 and moved his Imperial Pool Hall into it. Despite the distant connection between the Louvre and the Imperial, there is no disputing the fact that the Imperial had its dispensary license a mere five-and-a-half weeks after prohibition ended. (In the course of my research, I have found no other bar in Alaska still doing business today that received a license earlier than the Imperial.) Stocker was born in Switzerland in 1874 and was living in Fairbanks in 1910. He made extensive renovations to the Louvre (now Stocker) building in 1933 and 1935 and owned the Imperial until 1944. He died in 1955 and is buried in the Evergreen Cemetery in Juneau.

The Imperial was also known as the Imperial Cigar Store, the Imperial Pool Parlor, and the Imperial Pool Hall, which was the name used until 1952. That year, John "Potts" Pasquan and Joe Brignole sold it to Joe McNallen, who also owned the Arctic Bar in Juneau. McNallen changed the name to the Imperial Billiards and Bar. In 1963, McNallen sold it to Robert and Vivian Schroth.

The Schroth's owned and managed the Imperial for thirty-five years. Unfortunately, the bar became a hangout for a seedier element; there were several drug busts and many disorderly conduct arrests. In 1996, the Juneau Assembly almost blocked the liquor license renewal because of the frequent law violations. Robert "Rob" Daniels bought the Imperial from the Schroth's in 1998 and began a successful campaign to clean up the Imperial.

> **Visiting the Imperial Bar**: Whether you are a tourist or a local, you'll know you're in an historic pool hall when you step inside the Imperial. The stamped tin ceiling is the original, and the wooden floors and walls, along with

a noticeable lack of windows add to the historic feel. In the front of the bar, facing the street, are actual garage doors that Daniels raises during the summer months. July 3 and New Years Eve are the busiest days of the year.

"SNOOKER'S my game," says John D. Pasquan of Imperial Billiards, as he watches a Juneau pool expert.

From Tewkesbury's Alaska Business Directory, Travel Guide & Almanac – 1948. *By William Tewkesbury*

Bubble Room Lounge
127 North Franklin Street, Juneau
(907) 586-2662

License Issued: January 1, 1939, to the Baranof Hotel, Inc.
Amenities: TV's, food.
Find them Online: Facebook (TheBubbleRoomBaranof)

History and Notoriety: Architect Don McDonald envisioned in his plans for the luxurious Baranof Hotel "a unique tavern room." Unique is a good descriptor of this hotel bar, which has been the scene of countless political meetings that spawned historic decisions affecting Alaska. The Alaska Statehood Act, the Alaska Native Claims Settlement Act, the Alaska National Interest Lands Conservation Act, to name just a few, were discussed and argued, over drinks, at the Bubble Room. Opening night was March 10, 1939.

Joseph Driscoll, in his book *War Discovers Alaska* described the Bubble Room of 1943. "Visitors to the Baranof are sometimes puzzled by a sign reading 'No Stagging In The Bubble Room.' Investigation develops that this is not a prohibition against shooting deer, but a reminder that gentlemen unaccompanied by ladies must not pass from the bar into the adjoining room which is designated as the Bubble Room and is equipped with a juke box, booths, soft lights, and a small, waxed floor for dancing. There are no bubble dancers and no cover charge and, positively, no stags."

Before long, the focus of the Bubble Room changed from a supper club and dance destination to politics. In his book *Growing up in Alaska*, former Lieutenant Governor John "Jack" Coghill described his time as a member of the territorial house during the 1950s. After sessions were over "a lot of them would go down to the Bubble Room in the Baranof Hotel and have meetings, although some of us used to call it the Trouble Room at the Bourbonof Hotel!"

Lewis Lapham, the former editor of *Harper's Magazine*, visited Juneau in 1970 for a story about Alaska's oil bonanza and how the state was going to spend the billions of dollars coming in. For his piece *Alaska: Politicians and Natives, Money and Oil*, Lapham spent quality time in the Bubble Room, primarily because it was, and still is, a gathering spot for lawmakers and lobbyists.

☛**Visiting the Bubble Room:** There are no signs that announce that you have arrived at the famous Bubble Room, but it's easy enough to find on the first floor of the Baranof. The painting behind the bar of a poker game is by artist Don Clever and has been in the hotel since it opened.

Have a hamburger and a cocktail and keep your eyes and ears open as the chances of seeing a mover and a shaker are good, particularly when the State Legislature is in session from January through April.

From Alaska Life *magazine* – October 1947.

The Sandbar
(a.k.a. Sandbar and Grille)
2525 Industrial Boulevard, Juneau
(907) 789-8400

License issued: November 27, 1981, to Lloyd G. and Gail (Hildre) Niemi, and Lee Whiteman
Amenities: Pool table, foosball, darts, TVs, food, occasional live music
Find them Online: https://sandbarjuneau.com/; Facebook

History and Notoriety: Lloyd "Jerry" Niemi was born in Juneau in 1945. After high school, he joined the Army and served two years in Vietnam. He lived in Seattle and worked as a musician before returning to Juneau. In 1981, he married Gail Hildre who was also from Juneau. That same year, they opened The Sandbar which was first located at 2055 Jordan Ave. but moved to its current location in 1988.

Jerry was diagnosed with cancer in 2020 but was still able to drive himself to The Sandbar to visit his friends. He would say "Every day is a gift, that's why it's called the present!" He passed away in 2021. The Niemi family still owns the bar.

☛**Visiting The Sandbar:** The Sandbar is more of a bar than a restaurant, but it is known for its food, specifically deep-fried halibut served with chips (French fries). The recipe came from the Thane Ore House, a gone but not-forgotten Juneau restaurant. If you want to have a beer or cocktail with your food, you'll need to sit in the bar. The Sandbar does a pig roast on New Years Day.

Squirez
(a.k.a. Squires Rest)
11806 Glacier Highway, Juneau
(907) 789-7829

License Name Change Issued: April 1973 to David A. Horton Jr.

Amenities: Pool tables, darts, TVs, food, occasional live entertainment

Find them Online: Facebook

History and Notoriety: Squirez has its roots in a bar known as The After Hours, owned by Gary W. Horton, which opened here in 1967. The Horton family moved to Juneau from Chicago in 1946. Horton's Hardware opened in 1947 on the first floor of this building. The After Hours, located upstairs, occupied the former family home.

In 1971, Horton transferred the liquor license to his brother David, who changed the name to The Squire's Rest in 1973. In 1996, the building and bar were sold to Donald and Diane Howell, who temporarily changed the name to the Auke Bay Inn. In 2000, Howell leased the bar to Troy Cunningham and Brandon Petaja, who brought back the Squires Rest name. Squires Rest offered food in the form of Pappy Poes Pork Place.

Cunningham, also a musician, bought a six-inch long African house snake and named him "Rocks." Rocks was housed above the bar in a plastic container that included a wolf skull. The snake grew to be a few feet long and became a celebrity of sorts, who enjoyed loud rock and roll music. When the bar was sold to Shayla Weeks-Kaiser in 2012, she relocated Rocks into a large tank where the fireplace used to be. The eighteen-year-old Rocks died in 2019.

The bar, known as Squirez since 2014, is in a large room with a high ceiling that has been described as "cavernous." The bar has a beautiful view of Auke Bay, which can be stunning at sunset. In 2016, eight trees were planted at the harbor across the street from the bar which caused alarm for Squirez and the other businesses in the building that didn't want the view to be compromised. A "Save the View" campaign resulted in the relocation of the trees.

Celebrities who have visited Squirez include football great Tim Wrightman and baseball star Zach Plesac.

☞Visiting Squirez: While the view is a big draw, this is also the bar closest to the university. Dart players love the bar for its ten boards. Good food is available from The Anchor.

Harbor Bar
1 Main Street, Haines
(907) 766-2444

License Issued: 1954 to Olav Lillegraven
Amenities: Pool tables, TVs, occasional live entertainment, liquor store
Find them Online: Facebook

History and Notoriety: The Harbor Bar can trace its roots back to a bar known as The Gateway, which was located here in 1907. Owner Harry Brie advertised The Gateway as "The Best-Appointed Resort for Gentlemen in the North." The industrial-style building has always had the false front façade. During prohibition, the bar operated as a "card room" and during the 1940s the building housed a commissary and later a grocery. Olav Lillegraven, born in Norway, sold the bar to Charles and Betty Burnett in 1955.

"Charlie" Burnett was born in Kansas in 1922, served in WWII, and died at the Harbor Bar in 1966 at the young age of 42. His wife Betty sold the bar to Jack Martin in 1974, and it was Jack's wife Ramona who opened the Lighthouse restaurant in 1976.

Haines pioneer Carl Heinmiller talked about an incident in the early days of the Harbor Bar. The building is located over the old dock, and the bathroom sat directly out over the water. As there wasn't any plumbing, whatever fell went into a sump hole on the beach. When the tide came in, the toilet flushed. Someone went to the bathroom and dropped a cigarette which ignited some sawdust. Smoke soon filled the bar. The bartender set up about ten glasses, saying, "The place is burning down. Drink up." Most customers ran out except Jim McGhee, a steady at the bar. He sat on the foot rail and reached over his head to grab a glass and gulp it down. He continued down the foot rail in a seated position reaching for glass after glass. Meanwhile, a fire truck arrived equipped with a 100-pound pump. Fire Chief I.B. Howser ran down underneath the fire onto the beach and fell into the sump hole. Poor Howser was yelling "Pull me out of here" which Heinmiller did. Howser screamed to the guy with the high-pressure hose, "Don't stand there. Wash me off!" The young fireman holding the nozzle did as he was told, projecting a force of icy cold water that rolled Chief Howser down the beach.

The building has been expanded several times, including adding the section in the rear which now houses the Lighthouse Restaurant. The interior of the bar has a beautiful old mahogany back bar that might date back to The Gateway days.

☞**Visiting the Harbor Bar:** The location of the Harbor Bar commands a spectacular view of Lynn Canal, with some of the best views from the Lighthouse restaurant. Inside are many framed photos of fishing vessels and former patrons. Independence Day, Mardi Gras in September, and Halloween are popular times at the Harbor Bar.

From Lou Jacobin's Guide to Alaska and the Yukon *– 1958.*

Fogcutter Bar
122 Main Street, Haines
(907) 766-2555

License Issued: August 5, 1983, to Robert E. Vill
Amenities: Pool tables, TVs, food
Find them Online: https://www.fogcutterbar.com; Facebook

History and Notoriety: In 1923, Erik Oslund constructed the building that currently houses the Fogcutter. Oslund Hardware was in business until 1980 when Donald "Duck" Hess bought the building and moved his Rip Tide Bar into it. In 1983, Bob and Dorothy Vill bought the Rip Tide and renamed it the Fogcutter. Before marrying Bob, Dorothy was the wife of the late Bill Sweeney, who owned Sweeney's Corner Bar in Juneau. Brian and Linda Lemcke bought the Fogcutter in 1987, and their nephew Kelly Jessup bought the bar in 2015.

The Fogcutter is the place to be before and after the Alcan 200. Beginning in 1969, the Alcan 200 is known as the "longest snowmachine road race in North America." Held on a Saturday in January or February, all racers must register at the Fogcutter. The event attracts Americans and Canadians who vie for a $1,500 first prize. The night before the race, a Calcutta auction is held at the Fogcutter, which can get pretty lively.

The Kluane-Chilkat International Bike Relay, held in June, is another popular event where many of the competitors celebrate the finish at the Fogcutter.

☛**Visiting the Fogcutter Bar:** The Fogcutter attracts an assortment of locals and tourists. The outdoor beer garden is popular with bikers during the summer. Live music can be found here on weekends, and the pizza is excellent. Other popular times to be at the Fogcutter are Independence Day and during the Haines Labor Day Mardi Gras celebration.

Pioneer Bar (Haines)
13 Second Avenue, Haines
(907) 766-3443

License Issued: June 22, 1933, to Andree DeMoore
Amenities: Pool table, TVs, Bamboo Room Restaurant
Find them Online: https://bamboopioneer.net/; Facebook

History and Notoriety: The building that houses the Pioneer was built in the 1890s and was operating as the Hotel de France from 1904 to 1922. Andree Moore (a.k.a. Andree DeMoore; a.k.a. Lou LaMoore) was born in France in 1894 and immigrated to the U.S. in 1904. She was a prostitute and an enterprising madam, and had managed hookers in Anchorage, Seward, and Juneau. In 1933 she moved to Haines where she obtained a dispensary license and opened the Pioneer Beer Parlor and Restaurant, with a brothel upstairs. Moore married John Wierenga; a US Army soldier stationed in Haines. The couple divorced in 1941 and both left Alaska. In 1950, Moore and her new husband Fred Hamilton owned a restaurant named Andree's in San Jose, California, where she died in 1956. Dave and Margaret Fenton took over the Pioneer in 1943 having previously owned the Columbia Bar in Sitka. The Fenton' renamed it the Pioneer Cocktail Lounge. J.B. Carlyle owned the bar in 1945, and Florence Raney bought it in 1951. Raney sold it to Martin "Marty" Tengs in 1954. The Tengs family have owned and operated the Pioneer ever since.

Tengs was born in 1919 in Oregon, moved to Sitka in 1940, and Haines in 1952. He insisted on good liquor and proper grammar while presiding over card games, chess matches, parties and politics at the Pioneer Bar for almost forty years. His poker games were a hallmark of the bar. He also served as Mayor of Haines for two years. In 1991 Tengs transferred ownership of the bar to his daughter Christine (Christy) who now co-owns it with her husband Bob Fowler. Marty Tengs passed away in 2000.

An addition on the left side of the building was once a card room with dice tables. Tengs rented the room to Fran Fox, who hung a bamboo curtain that created two rooms, and opened the Bamboo Room Restaurant. Today the Bamboo Room is renowned for its deep-fried halibut and chips.

☛**Visiting the Pioneer Bar:** No trip to Haines is complete without a visit to the Pioneer. The distinctive red, two-story building with a false front and the mural of Tengs and his past customers on the right side is easy to find. Be sure to check out the ceiling tiles. Sporting events on the big screen, the Great Alaska Beer Craft Festival on Memorial Day weekend, and Mardi Gras on Labor Day weekend are prime times at the Pioneer.

Andree and John Wierenga.
Photo courtesy of Christy Tengs Fowler

Red Onion Saloon
201 Broadway, Skagway
(907) 983-2222

License Issued: June 22, 1980, to Jan Wrentmore
Amenities: Brothel Museum, food
Find them Online: https://www.redonion1898.com/; Facebook

History and Notoriety: Peter Lawson, a Seattle saloon man, built the Red Onion in the fall of 1898. The two-story wood structure was first located at the corner of Sixth Avenue and State Street. The Red Onion was, for about one year, Skagway's largest dance hall and saloon. The upstairs brothel was first class compared to the cribs on Yokohama Row and Paradise Alley.

Dr. Catherine Spude did an exhaustive study of the gold rush saloons of Skagway in a National Park Service publication titled *The Mascot Saloon*. According to Spude, the Red Onion was renamed The Senate in 1900. One year later, it was going by the name of The Seattle, and by 1903, it was The Totem. By 1905, the population of Skagway had dwindled so much that The Totem closed.

In 1914, the building was moved to its current location using just one horse. Unfortunately, it was dragged backwards and the front and back of the building had to be removed to switch them. Skagway voted itself dry in 1916, and the building was used over the years as an army barracks, a laundry, a bakery, a union hall, a TV station, and a gift shop.

In 1976, the entire town of Skagway became a National Historic Landmark. Two years later, Jan Wrentmore, a former public relations officer, bought the building and reopened the Red Onion Saloon on July 4, 1980. In 1998, Wrentmore spent $250,000 to restore the building to be authentic as possible. The upstairs is now a museum that invites tourists to view a genuine nineteenth century brothel.

In May 1994, the cast and crew of the TV show *Good Morning America* came to Alaska and visited Skagway. Weatherman Spencer Christian was filmed inside the Red Onion drinking an Alaskan Amber beer. Spenser was known for his quips and used "Let's see what's brewing in the weather" and "Sometimes it's unbeerable."

☛**Visiting the Red Onion Saloon:** Expect lots of cruise ship tourists during the summer months. The building restoration was a success, and the attractive young ladies decked out in 1898 period costumes add a great deal of charm. Independence Day and Soapy Smith's Wake on July 8th are popular times at the Red Onion. This bar is open only from April – October.

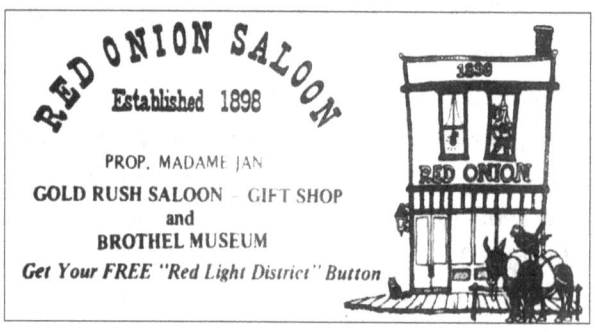

Ad from the Skaguay Alaskan – Summer 1980.

Glass Door Bar
550 Mallott Avenue, Yakutat
(907) 784-3331

License Issued: 1973 to Yakutat Community Corporation
Amenities: Pool table, TVs, occasional live music, liquor store
Find them Online: Facebook

History and Notoriety: The Glass Door has always been simply a bar and liquor store and not part of a restaurant or lodge. The bar takes its name from a glass door that was part of the original entrance. Too many nights of clumsy or aggressive clients revealed the impracticality of the ornate feature.

In 1990, an article in the *Anchorage Daily News* described a local fishing guide named Frank Deveraux, who was known in Yakutat for his combat style of fishing. Deveraux was also known to have a violent temper when drinking and had a reputation for verbal and physical altercations at the Glass Door. His behavior earned him a "banned for life" sentence from Evelyn Anderson, who managed the Glass Door in the 1980s and '90s.

The bar has burned down and been re-built at least twice. Patrons have also "accidentally" driven their vehicles into the front of the building on multiple occasions. A barricade in the form of logs and later a deck has become a permanent fixture.

In recent years, Yakutat has become famous for its world class fishing and for its waves. During the spring and fall months, it is not uncommon for the crowd at the Glass Door to consist of fishermen, surfers, hunters, wildlife photographers, and scientists studying the Hubbard Glacier.

> **Visiting the Glass Door Bar:** There is no sign announcing that you have arrived at the Glass Door. The weekly poker tournaments are a big draw. Independence Day, Fairweather Day on August first, the annual Fishermen's Party at the end of September, Halloween and New Years Eve are other popular times to be there.

From Lou Jacobin's Guide to Alaska and the Yukon *– 1954, The Pinzon, 302 McKinley Street, Old Valdez 1934-1964, 129 Tatitlek, New Valdez 1964-1988.*

NOTORIOUS BARS OF SOUTHCENTRAL ALASKA

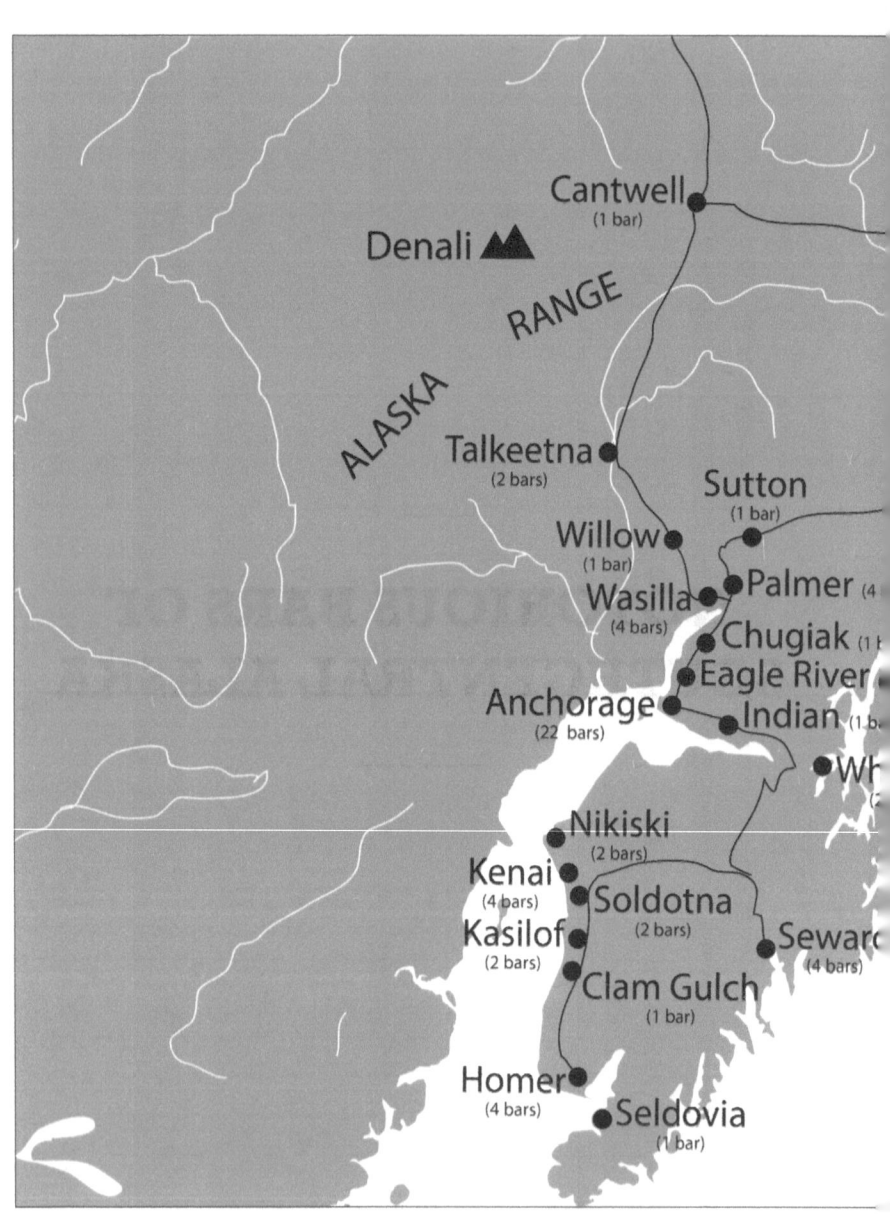

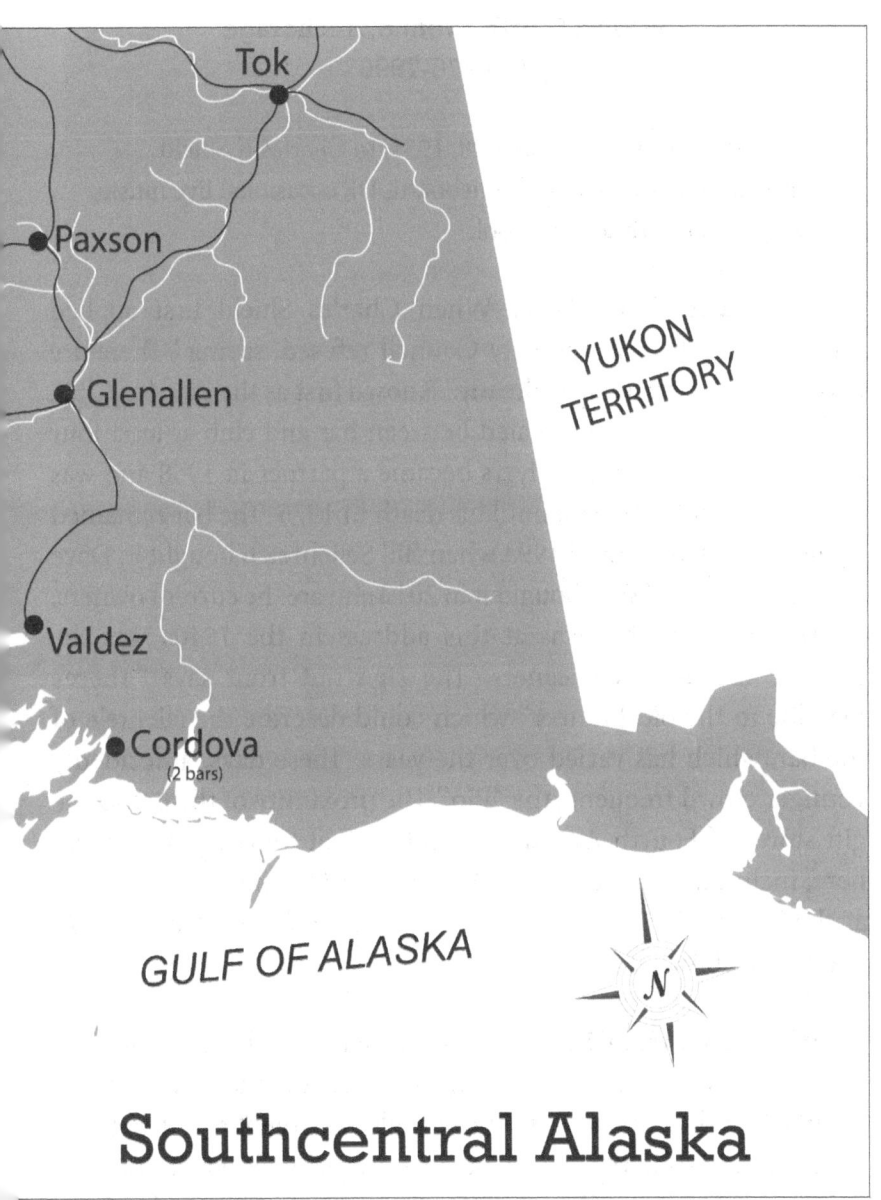

Southcentral Alaska

Pioneer Bar
(Anchorage; a.k.a. The Pio)
739 West Fourth Avenue, Anchorage
(907) 276-7996

License Issued: December 28, 1951, to Charles F. Shield
Amenities: Pool tables, shuffleboard, DJ, occasional live music
Find them Online: Facebook

History and Notoriety: When Charles Shield first applied for the liquor license, the City Council refused, saying "There are enough bars on that block already." Known first as the Pioneer Club, the official name has alternated between bar and club at least four times in its history. Noel Myers became a partner in 1958 and was the sole owner from 1966 until his death in 1976. The bar remained in the Myers family until 1993 when Bill Seltenreich bought it. Dave Croffut and Mike Ward bought it in 2013 and are the current owners.

The business that was at this address in the 1940s was the Pioneer Laundry & Cleaners. The sign out front says "There's new life in the old Pioneer" which could describe the clientele of the bar, which has varied over the years. These days, a decidedly younger crowd frequents the "Pio." The proximity of the bar to the gift stores of Fourth Avenue guarantees that tourists will also be here, including Jeff Corwin of Animal Planet fame, who hung out at the Pio in 2006 while filming his *Into Alaska with Jeff Corwin* reality TV show.

> **Visiting the Pioneer Bar:** The bar is on the small side and is guaranteed to be packed on the weekends. Framed black-and-white photos on the walls document significant time periods in the history of Anchorage. The Pioneer touts itself as being the "home of the almost perfect bartenders." Ladies be forewarned: there is only one toilet. If there is a wait, you can always dart four doors down to the Gaslight.

Gaslight Lounge
721 West Fourth Avenue, Anchorage
(907) 277-0722

License Issued: 1970 to Michael, Phillip and William O'Neill
Amenities: Pool tables, darts, TVs, occasional live music

History and Notoriety: Henry "Harry" O'Neill added a cocktail bar and liquor store to Richmond's Cafe at this location in 1940. Harry was born in North Dakota in 1885 but was living in Cordova in 1908. With his sons Michael "Mike" and Francis "Jack" he would also own the Victory Bar in Anchorage and the Alpine Inn in Sutton. Richmond's survived the 1964 earthquake with minimal damage, which prompted Mike to set up a table with free food and drinks. The O'Neills sold the bar license in 1967 and maintained just the liquor store, known as the Brown Jug. In 1970, Mike and his sons bought the license back and re-opened the bar, renaming it the Gaslight.

A. Einer "Bud" Hagberg and his wife Bernice bought the Gaslight in 1975. Bud worked for Wien Airlines for thirty-one years, retiring in 1977 to focus on the bar. He passed away that same year. Bernice continued to manage the Gaslight until she sold it to John Pattee in 1991.

A 2011 article in the *Anchorage Press* about haunted places in Anchorage included the Gaslight. The day manager stated that he had worked at the bar for twenty years. He spoke of loud noises inside the bar and on the roof when no one else was around, and said the jukebox would suddenly start playing songs from the 1940s and '50s, selected by unseen hands. Ghost tours of downtown Anchorage always stop at the Gaslight.

☞**Visiting the Gaslight Lounge:** The comely female bartenders are friendly and generous. The Gaslight has enough room for a mechanical bull and a stripper pole (no nudity allowed). Weekends are also a good time to listen to live music here (usually rock); DJ's keep the place rockin' the rest of the week.

From Lou Jacobin's Guide to Alaska and the Yukon – 1971.

Darwin's Theory
426 G Street, Anchorage
(907) 277-5322

License Issued: September 4, 1981, to Darwin Biwer, Jr., Dick Delak, and Bill Seltenreich
Amenities: TV's, jukebox, popcorn
Find them Online: https://www.alaska.net/~thndrths/; Facebook

History and Notoriety: Back in 1970, the bar/restaurant that was at this location was known as Ruthie's 49er. Darwin Biwer grew up in Salem, Oregon, moved to Alaska in 1966, worked as a fishery biologist for fifteen years, and decided to buy the 49er from seventy-six-year-old Ruth "Ruthie" Sutton. After extensive renovations, the bar opened with Biwer as bartender, a job he performed for the first eleven years. At the time, co-owner Dick "Birdhouse" Delak owned the infamous Bird House Bar on Turnagain Arm.

Biwer recalled when comedian Dave Attell visited and filmed inside the bar several late summer nights in 2002 as part of his *Insomniac* TV show. Biwer told Attell that the bartenders had compiled a collection of Polaroid photos of customers (and bartenders, too)—usually in a state of undress. Attell was intrigued, and the "Boob Book" became a focal point of his visit. The Darwin's Theory Boob Book has been missing in action for years now.

Darwin's has been repeatedly voted as the "Best Dive Bar" in Anchorage by readers of the *Anchorage Daily News*. The amenities are few, but the atmosphere is always electric. The all-female bartenders are flirty and efficient. The only time I've ever been in a bar when someone rang the bell (known as "timbering the bar" and meaning that all drinks are courtesy of the ringer) happened in Darwin's, twice in one night! Lucky that my friends and I were there the same week that the Permanent Fund dividend checks were being sent out.

☞**Visiting the Darwin's Theory:** Darwin's claims to be the world's biggest seller of Dekuyper cinnamon schnapps, and the house drink is called a "Red Hot" (cinnamon schnapps with a dash of Tabasco). The bar observes all the usual celebration days, but the annual Easter "Eggstravaganza" egg-coloring contest is a riot! Arrive early and know that it will be standing room only.

Darwin inside his bar. Photo courtesy of Darwin Biwer

Bernie's Bungalow Lounge
(a.k.a. Bernie's)
626 D Street, Anchorage
(907) 276-8808

License issued: December 5, 1997, to Bernard Souphanavong
Amenities: Food, occasional live entertainment
Find them Online: http://www.bernieslounge.com/; Facebook

History and Notoriety: Bernard "Bernie" Souphanavong was born in 1951 in the country of Laos. Parts of Laos had been occupied by the North Vietnamese since 1958, making it a key part of the Vietnam War. The war ended in 1975, and Bernie moved to Alaska that same year. He was naturalized in Anchorage in 1980. For a few years he was the man in charge of Chinese takeout food at the Carrs grocery stores. He also owned a tofu and sprout company.

In 1993, he opened Bernie's Bar and Grill in the Mall at Sears on Northern Lights Blvd. It became known as a dinner and jazz club. In 1997, he bought a house on D Street that had been the Pickle Barrel Deli and opened Bernie's. In 1998, he changed the name to The Bungalow Lounge.

Bernie's began as an indoor 2-story lounge that served martinis, displayed modern art and sculptures, and had dim lighting in the corners. It quickly expanded to the outdoor patio, and then to the entire yard, with tables under umbrellas and a stage. In 2008, Bernie's hosted the Summer Solstice House of Hip-Hop, a five-day event with each night themed around a different element of hip-hop music.

Bernie was a man interested in people, music, and food. In 2016, he submitted thousands of signatures to run for Congress as an independent. While he didn't win, he continued to live his life, and to travel around the world. Back at home, he wore silk robes, latex, loafers, hats, and jewelry. He passed away in 2021. His son Brandon is now the owner.

☛**Visiting Bernie's Bungalow**: This is one of my favorite bars in Anchorage. I'm happy to sit inside the snug house with the comfy chairs, at the bar, or outside on the spacious patio. Craft cocktails are a good choice here.

Bernie crafting a cocktail. From Bernie's Bungalow Lounge *Facebook page*

The Avenue
(a.k.a. The Ave)
338 West Fourth Avenue, Anchorage
(907) 272-6124

License Name Change Issued: May 8, 1984, to Richard and John Pattee
Amenities: Pool table, darts, TV's, food, occasional live music
Find them Online: https://avenuebarak.com/; Facebook

History and Notoriety: The Avenue has its roots in a bar known as the Union Club, which was at this location from 1941 – 1984. The Union Club was not only a cocktail bar, but also offered pool, cards, a café and liquor store. To many old-time Alaskans, it was an institution, and a home to the "sourdoughs." In 1964, the Union Club was one of five bars, including the Panhandle, on the south side of the 300 block of Fourth Avenue that survived the earthquake with minimal damage, in stark contrast to the north side of the block.

By the early 1980s, the older clientele was gone. In 1983, Richard Pattee and his son John bought the bar and changed the name the following year. The bar itself didn't change much, although anything that said Union Club on it was removed. Union Club tokens, ash trays, matchbooks, and other items can still be found on eBay.

Just like it's neighbor the Panhandle, the Avenue Bar has a history of violations, mostly over-service or allowing already drunk people to enter the bar. However, in 2006, the Avenue performed a major makeover, including hiring new staff, putting pine-colored paneling over the black walls, and adding couches, bar games, TV's and drink specials. This resulted in attracting younger, possibly less dicey patrons. John Pattee sold the bar to Robert Shafer and Logan Rammell in 2012.

In recent years, the Avenue has been the starting point for the Pride Bar Crawl, held every year in June.

☛**Visiting The Avenue**: While the ceiling is still black, the painted walls—some with murals—and the wood floor are bright and welcoming. The Avenue is a fun and interesting bar housed in a truly historic location.

Panhandle Bar
(a.k.a. The Pan)
312 West Fourth Avenue, Anchorage
(907) 277-9311

License Issued: 1933 to James R. Campbell
Amenities: Pool tables, darts, TV's, patio
Find them Online: Facebook

History and Notoriety: In the summer of 1915, Anchorage was a tent city that included a business known as The Panhandle. From early photos and newspaper ads, we know that Panhandle owner Tex Jones sold cigars, tobacco, and soft drinks. During the 1920s, owner Chauncey Peterson reportedly also sold his customers moonshine. By December of 1933, Jim Campbell was legally selling beer at the Panhandle. The bar, which is still located at the exact same address, is undoubtedly the oldest in continuous operation in Anchorage (not counting license suspensions) and is one of the oldest bars in Alaska.

As early as 1946, the Panhandle was recognized as the oldest bar in town by the *Anchorage Daily Times*. The same article reported that the bar received an unsanitary rating by a health inspector, a ruling which suspended the liquor license. More license suspensions were to come over the years, usually for violations like selling to a minor or for over-service (serving people who are already intoxicated). The reputation of the bar suffered more in 2006 when Anchorage police working undercover made seven drug buys in two months in or around the bar. According to articles published in the *Anchorage Daily News*, the police said that customers referred to the bar as "the Crack Handle." The bar owners, who denied the allegations, felt that the bar was being unfairly targeted by the Anchorage Assembly, and particularly by then Mayor Mark Begich. So many sting operations targeted the Panhandle that the owners had a black and yellow sign created that showed a wasp projecting its stinger, with the words "Panhandle Bar Stingers."

A persistent rumor says that there was once an underground tunnel that connected the Panhandle with the Union Club (now The Avenue Bar) a few doors down. Both bars survived the 1964 earthquake with a minimum amount of damage. However, evidence of the tunnel has not been found. In the 1950s, an after-hours club known as the Silver Slipper operated in the basement of the Panhandle. Jazz pianist (and later music professor) Wendy

Williamson, after whom the large auditorium on the University of Alaska Anchorage campus is named, was a performer there.

☞**Visiting the Panhandle Bar:** Despite its seedy reputation, the Panhandle is worthy of a visit, simply because of its historic value. Note the old cash register and the revolving nude woman above the bar. Come for a drink during the day if it makes you feel safer, as you're not as likely to encounter the loyal but possibly somewhat rougher clientele.

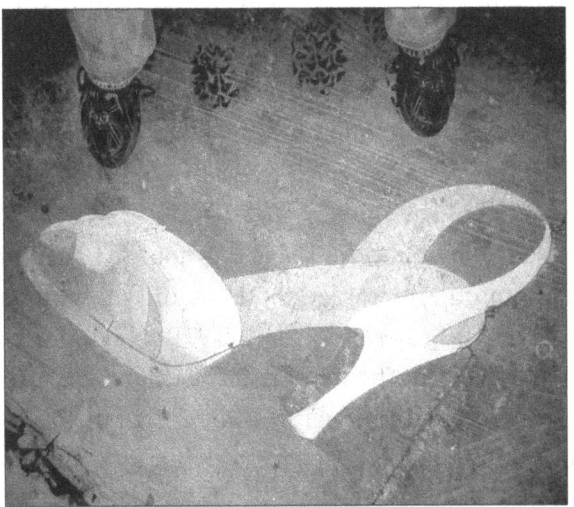

Silver Slipper image on the basement floor of the Panhandle Bar. Photo by the author – 2015

Polar Bar
507 East Fifth Avenue, Anchorage
(907) 279-0869

License Issued: 1950 to Floyd Wacha
Amenities: Pool tables, darts, shuffleboard, TV's
Find them Online: Facebook

History and Notoriety: This bar was first known as the Polar Bar-r and was located at 427 Fourth Avenue. It moved to its current location in 1965.

For many years, the theme of the Polar Bar was polar bears. In the early 1990s, then owner Louis Vukmir hired local artist Bob Patterson to paint images of polar bears playing golf that decorated the bar. In 1995, Patterson painted the impressive "History of Anchorage" mural on the side of the building at 645 G Street.

In 1969, a bartender on duty and a professional dancer were shot in the Polar Bar. Both survived. The man guilty of the crime was sentenced to 40 years but was out on parole after only seven years. In 1970, a safe weighing several hundred pounds and containing over a thousand dollars was taken from the Polar Bar. It was found later the same day with the money missing. A teenage male was convicted of the crime.

One thing the owners of the Polar Bar couldn't have predicted was that the Sheraton Anchorage Hotel would be built catty-corner to the bar, opening their doors in 1979. Having a notorious bar across the street from the hotel hasn't escaped the attention of out-of-town guests, including actor and comedian Eddie Griffin, who stopped by the Polar in 2011 for a drink and to mingle with the locals.

> **Visiting the Polar Bar:** Curious tourists from the Sheraton wander in during the summer months, but the Polar is primarily a local's bar. In addition to the remaining polar bear paintings above the bar, notice the vintage cigarette machine, and the carvings.

Mad Myrna's
(a.k.a. Myrna's)
530 East Fifth Avenue, Anchorage
(907) 276-9762

License Name Change Issued: October 29, 1998, to Don Chinn (Club Chinatown, Inc.)
Amenities: Food, live entertainment
Find them Online: https://madmyrnas.com/; Facebook

History and Notoriety: Mad Myrna's has its roots in Club Chinatown, a nightclub that was at this location in 1966. Don Chinn was born in China in 1922, moved to Seattle with his father in 1935, and found work in restaurants. When WWII broke out, he enlisted in the Navy and was sent to Alaska and then Japan. After the war, he got married and moved back to Alaska.

In 1954, Chinn opened Don's Café at Fifteenth and Gambell in Anchorage. Two years later, he moved the café to 528 East Fifth Ave., renamed it Don's Green Apple, and got a liquor license in 1963. In 1966, he opened Club Chinatown next door to the café. He sold the club in 1971, and it became the Pierce Street Annex in 1975. He bought it back in 1986 and renamed it the Alaska Permanent Fun Annex. In 1988, he closed the café and combined both businesses into the Blue Moon Lounge and Disco, the first gay bar in Anchorage with a drag show. In an interview for the *Anchorage Daily News* in 1994, he described the discrimination he experienced as a Chinese American, and how he identified with gay people. "I was uneasy with a lot of places I could not go, and there's a lot of places the gay were not welcome. I open the gay bar so the gay people be free and have a home for themselves."

In 1996, he followed a national trend and changed the Blue Moon into a bar and restaurant called the Alaska Blues. Two years later, he returned to the gay bar and drag show theme, naming the bar Mad Myrna's after a local drag queen. The bar had dance music every night of the week and drag shows on Friday nights. Myrna's also sponsored the Mr./Ms./Miss Gay Alaska Pageant, and the Duke and Duchess Ball. This led to full-on musical productions like *Cabaret*, the *Rocky Horror Picture Show*, *Little Shop of Horrors*, and *Debbie Does Dallas*. The drag shows were also expanded to appeal to a wider (straight) audience and are now both Friday and Saturday nights.

Chinn passed away in 2003. His daughter Linda took over until 2019, when Tim and Rebeckah Lyons bought Myrna's.

☛**Visiting Mad Myrna's:** Myrna's continues to be welcoming to all and is a great place to dance. Friday Night Divas can be packed, as are events during Pride Week in June, especially the Drag Queen Bingo. Halloween at Myrna's is a highly costumed affair. Reservations are encouraged.

Van's Dive Bar
(a.k.a. Van's; a.k.a. King's X)
1027 East Fifth Avenue, Anchorage
(907) 929-5464

License Issued: November 14, 1967, to Harold Brown
Amenities: Pool tables, darts, TVs, food, live music
Find them Online: https://www.vansdivebaralaska.com/; Facebook

History and Notoriety: In 1965, this was the location of Rosetta's Cocktail Lounge. In 1967, Harold Brown bought Rosetta's and changed the name to King's X (pronounced "King's Cross"). During the oil boom years, the King's X had a boxing ring on one side and a movie screen on the other, where 8 mm movies were shown. The King's X was one of the first bars people saw when entering Anchorage on the Glenn Highway.

The Kings X changed hands several times in forty-nine years until Van Hale (of The Marx Bros Cafe fame) and his wife Nicki Shinners bought the bar in 2016. The couple changed the name to Van's Dive Bar. Although some people might still refer to the bar as the King's X, the bar has been given a "facelift" according to Shinners, which includes repairing holes in the walls, and refurbishing the bathrooms.

> **Visiting Van's Dive Bar:** This bar now shines in ways that the old King's X never did but hasn't lost the dive bar feel. Van's features regular live music. The April 2023 "Vanniversary" celebration featured twenty-eight musical acts (!).

Barry's Baranof Lounge
1166 Gambell Street, Anchorage
(907) 276-9042

License Issued: 1964 to Wilfred Joinette and Robert Inglis
Amenities: Pool table, darts, TVs, occasional live music
Find them Online: Facebook

History and Notoriety: In 1978, Herman Angel and Charles Bannister bought the Baranof and then sold it to Carl Higdon in 1981. Higdon added Barry Tanner as a partner in the venture in 1982. Tanner bought out Higdon that same year, changing the name to Barry's Baranof Lounge in 1988.

Tanner, from California, was raised in Oregon, and moved to Anchorage in 1967. He managed Barry's Baranof until 2014 when he passed away.

In the early 1980s, the Baranof was also known as "Menopause Manor" because it was frequented by older women looking for younger men, patrons that might be called "cougars" these days.

☛**Visiting Barry's Baranof**: The Baranof is dark and divey but is a great place to have a drink before or after attending an event at the nearby Sullivan Arena.

Barry Tanner (1945 – 2014). Photo courtesy of Heidi Tidler

Crossroads Lounge
1402 Gambell Street, Anchorage
(907) 279-7218

License Issued: 1952 to Damon Polk
Amenities: Pool table, darts, TVs, occasional live music
Find them Online: https://www.thecrossroadslounge.com/; Facebook

History and Notoriety: The Crossroads (also spelled Cross Roads) Lounge was originally located at 125 Fourth Avenue. James "Jimmie" Sumpter bought the bar in 1955 and moved it to its current location after the 1964 earthquake. M.C. Fuller and Jack Griffin bought the Crossroads in 1971 and then sold it to A. Einar "Bud" Hagberg and Carl Burnett the following year. The bar was sold to Don and Nan Skewis in 1983.

According to an interview with bartender Rosemary Burnett in the book *Last Call!* by Richard Robinson, the Crossroads was a hangout for ironworkers in the 1970s. There was a big glass Budweiser ball on the roof of the bar, and the men were always talking about shooting it with their pistols. After months of listening to this idle talk, she told them to just "shoot the son of a bitch" which they promptly did.

In 2002, a man was shot and killed inside the entryway to Crossroads, for no apparent reason. The alleged murderer died in prison before being tried for the crime.

In 2000 and 2003, Scott Gomez, the veteran National Hockey League center who was born and raised in Anchorage, brought the Stanley Cup to the Crossroads. The Crossroads was the favorite watering hole of Gomez' father. Many people stood in line to take a gulp of beer from hockey's holy grail.

➧Visiting Crossroads Lounge: The big brown log cabin with the red roof has two levels, which provides a spacious place to party before or after an event at the Sullivan Arena. The motto of the bar is "Where Friends Meet" and it is indeed a great place to meet up with friends who like watching sports, along with stiff drinks, cheap eats, and "feisty" bartenders.

Reilly's Irish Pub
(a.k.a. Cheechako Bar, a.k.a. Izzy's)
317 West Fireweed Lane, Anchorage
(907) 274-6132

License Issued: November 24, 1970, to Joseph and Margaret Reilly
Amenities: TVs, juke box, occasional live entertainment
Find them Online: Facebook

History and Notoriety: Joe Reilly, from New York City, came to Alaska in 1947. He worked as a mechanic and at the Mur-Mac Cocktail Lounge (now F Street Station). In 1952 he married Peggy, who was also Irish and from New York City. In 1958, they, along with Paul & June Lynch (also Irish) opened a bar across from Merrill Field named Pal Joey's. Pal Joey is the title of a 1957 Academy Award winning movie starring Frank Sinatra. The bar was advertised as the "Irish Coffee Haven" of the North.

In 1970, the Reillys opened The Cheechako Bar on then unpaved Fireweed Lane in a log cabin, which was previously the home of the Ebert family. The term (chee-CHA-koh) describes a newcomer to Alaska, usually someone who has not spent a winter here. The name was available because the Cheechako Tavern, which was at 441 Fourth Avenue in 1939, was destroyed by the 1964 earthquake. Paul and June took over Pal Joey's and renamed it the Irish Setter.

For many years, the Cheechako and the Irish Setter had a friendly competition as to which was the best Irish bar in town. Reilly installed neon shamrocks in the windows, loaded the jukebox with Irish music, served Harp and Guinness beer, and made sure his bartenders knew how to make a mean Irish Coffee. In fact, one of his bartenders, Isador "Izzy" Cordova, was twice voted "Best Bartender in Anchorage" by polls conducted by the *Anchorage Daily News*.

The Cheechako became known for its wild St. Patrick's Day parties, and as a good place to hold a wake. Reilly would boast that he introduced St. Patty's Day celebrations to Anchorage. The bar would serve hundreds (1,600 on one occasion) of free corned beef sandwiches, and feature dancers and bagpipers. The bar has seen more than its share of wakes and celebrations of life. The cozy atmosphere and mood lighting lend itself to intimate gatherings.

In 2005, Reilly sold the Cheechako to his daughter Jeanne and her husband Larry Bogue, who decided to honor him by changing the name of the bar to Reilly's. He was flattered, but even he continued to call the bar Cheechako. Peggy passed away in 2008, and Joe Reilly in 2012.

☛Visiting Reilly's: The Harp and Guinness are on tap now, and the jukebox is state-of-the-art, but this bar has retained the old time feel. The St. Patrick's Day parties are not to be missed (standing room only). Other notable parties are Halloween, the Repeal of Prohibition party, and the Celtic Winter Solstice Concert, both in December.

Joe Reilly (1922 – 2012). Photo courtesy of Jean Reilly Bogue

---

Koots
(a.k.a. Chilkoot Charlie's)
2435 Spenard Road, Anchorage
(907) 272-1010

License Issued: 1969 to Michael Gordon
Amenities: Pool tables, pinball, TVs, food, varied musical venues, live entertainment
Find them Online: https://www.koots.com/; Facebook

History and Notoriety: The bar that is known throughout Alaska (and the world) as Koots began as the Hitching Post, located here in 1951. The name was changed to Whitie's 2 X 4 in 1964, and then to the Alibi Club in 1968. Mike Gordon, who moved with his family to Alaska in 1953 and graduated from Anchorage High School in 1960, bought the Alibi Club and opened his "rustic Alaska saloon" on January 1, 1970. The mother of his partner Bill Jacobs loaned them twenty thousand dollars to get started.

The bar is named after a fictional, Alaskan sourdough character created by Ruben Gaines, a radio and television personality from Ketchikan. Gordon thought it would be a good name for his bar, and Gaines agreed to let him use it.

Koots is arguably the most famous bar in Alaska. It was once the most profitable, with annual revenues between $5 to 7 million. The bar initially occupied only the part of the building that is now the South Long Bar. The bar grew and popularity during the 1970s oil boom. During this period, the costumed bartenders entertained the crowds. Music was provided by the bar's original band, the Rinky-Dinks, and later by a piano player who called himself Mr. Whitekeys. Whitekeys left and opened his own bar, the Fly-By-Night Club, which was also on Spenard Road. It was Whitekeys who coined the Chilkoot Charlie's motto: "We cheat the other guy and pass the savings on to you!"

The bar eventually expanded into the adjacent buildings. Gordon spared no expense on entertainment either. Some of the many bands that have played at Koots include Metallica, the Steve Miller Band, Crosby Stills and Nash, Blues Traveler, Bon Jovi, Lynyrd Skynyrd, Ozzy Osbourne, the Beach Boys, Aerosmith, ZZ Top, Van Halen, and even Tiny Tim. Koots has been featured on *ESPN*, *Good Morning America*, *David Letterman* and the *Johnny Carson Show*. In 1989, actor Pauly Shore hosted an MTV Street Party here. In 2000, Koots was declared the #1 Bar in America by *Playboy* magazine.

In 2002, a replica of the Bird House Bar, once located on Turnagain Arm, was constructed inside Koots. It has the same slanted bar, juke box, lingerie and business cards on the walls, pickles, boneless chicken dinners, and even a Ptarmigan Horn. The only thing missing from the original bar is the musty smell.

Despite the financial success of the bar at this location, management problems doomed the spinoffs that opened in Fairbanks, Ester, and Girdwood. Gordon retired in 2015 and sold the bar to general manager Doran Powell and a group of longtime employees.

> **Visiting Koots:** I have probably spent more time, and money, in Koots than any other bar in Alaska. It has 8 bars (nine in the summertime). The South and North Long Bars still have sawdust covered floors, and padded tree stumps and beer kegs for seating. Check out the walls which are covered with photos and autographs from famous bands, beer can collections, and Alaska memorabilia. Koots is truly a must-see if you are visiting Anchorage. Be sure to check the online calendar and be prepared to wait in line on the weekends. Also, be aware that when entering you are being photographed. If you appear to be very happy (interpreted as drunk) you might not get in.

Buckaroo Club
(a.k.a. The Buck)
2811 Spenard Road, Anchorage
(907) 561-9251

License Issued: 1952 to James E. "Jimmie" Sumpter
Amenities: Pool tables, darts, shuffleboard, TVs
Find Them Online: Facebook

History and Notoriety: The word 'buckaroo' (or buckeroo) is another name for a cowboy or broncobuster, and the cowboy theme was in evidence here for many years. Jimmie Sumpter sold the bar to one of his bartenders, Reed "Dick" Dickey and his wife Jan in 1956. The building, which was constructed in 1948, survived the 1964 earthquake and over the years has seen hordes of customers two-stepping and waltzing to country music.

In 1955, two masked bandits held up Sumpter at the Buckaroo and escaped with five thousand dollars. In 1991, the Buckaroo Club was gutted by a fire. A much-beloved hefty calico cat named Ajax perished in the blaze.

Dickey passed away in 1980 and Jan in 1993. In 1996, the Dickey family sold the bar, and the new owners changed the name to Geno's. Two years later Michael Bell and Allen Cross bought the bar and brought back the Buckaroo name.

The location of the Buckaroo is at the northern end of a section of Spenard Road that in the 1970s and '80s had a string of massage parlors that were actually houses of prostitution. Just a couple blocks away was Cindy's Massage Parlor, owned by Johnny Rich, a mobster and the father of writer and teacher Kim Rich, who wrote a book about her experiences titled *Johnny's Girl*. As recently as 2005, an adult-oriented business next door to the Buckaroo was discovered to be engaging in prostitution.

☛Visiting the Buckaroo Club: The Buckaroo is a classic Alaska bar that celebrates its history. The bar sells t-shirts that proudly state "Buckaroo Club – Spenard AK – Est. 1953." Country music can still be heard here but rock is the new standard.

Jimmie Sumpter (1919 – 1993) from Lou Jacobin's Guide to Alaska – 1947.

Carousel Lounge
3206 Spenard Road, Anchorage
(907) 206-6001

License Issued: 1967 to Steve E. and Dorothy M. Cooper
Amenities: Pool tables, darts, TVs, food, occasional live music
Find Them Online: https://www.carouselalaska.com/; Facebook

History and Notoriety: The first Carousel bar in Anchorage, owned by James and Jessie Baker, opened in 1957 in a space upstairs at 232 Fourth Avenue. By 1963, it was no longer in business. The Carousel Lounge is a Spenard institution that has been doing business in the same location since 1967 (minus a two-year hiatus).

Steve and Dorothy "Tootie" Cooper, from Arkansas, married the same year that they opened the Carousel Lounge. During the pipeline days, the Carousel gained a reputation for catering to the wild and crazy crowd that also frequented the dozen or so massage parlors along this section of Spenard Road. The Carousel was (and is) very popular with bikers, and pool and dart teams made the bar their home base. A 1987 article in the *Anchorage Daily News* about dart teams in town touted "Carousel Lounge is generally acknowledged as the best men's team in the city, having dominated local competition for the last six years." The Cooper's sold the bar to Christopher Cox in 2003.

In 2005, Cox had a TV commercial made that was intended to improve the reputation of the bar. The low-budget commercial even showed a sleazy dude being tossed out the front door! Cox had the exterior of the building painted dark red with white stripes that mimicked a guitar that was owned by rock musician Eddie Van Halen. Citing declining sales and his own personal health issues, Cox closed the bar in 2016.

In early 2018, Paul Berger, a local businessman and self-described "happy landlord" bought the Carousel and hired Linda Bucinsky Coffer as manager. The Carousel has been given a serious makeover, which entailed Berger gutting the building, repainting the exterior, and installing wool carpet (originally from the Alaska Railroad) throughout the bar. Reopening day was April 20, 2018, a date that has been celebrated every year since.

☛**Visiting the Carousel Lounge:** This is a great place to listen to live music on the weekends (country, blues, rock, etc.). The Carousel celebrates all the usual occasions; be sure to check their website. The patio is a nice spot to be on a sunny day.

Time Out Lounge
4600 Old Seward Highway, Anchorage
(907) 562-2532

License Name Change Issued: March 5, 1976, to Louis LeQuire and Alfred Johnson
Amenities: Pool table, darts, TVs, food, occasional live music
Find them Online: Facebook

History and Notoriety: Louis "Lou" Le Quire and Alfred "Al" Johnson opened Lou's Lounge at this location in November of 1975. By March they had changed the name to the Time-Out, which is a common name for a bar but was a first for Alaska. In 1977 they sold the bar to William and Lorene Kalfas. Dave and Evelyn Randolph took over in 1987. Everyone called Evelyn "Midget" because she stood four-foot something and Dave was six-foot, five inches. The Randolph's owned the Time-Out until 2003. John "Icy" Ivanoff is the current owner.

In the book *Last Call!* by Richard Robinson, bartender Tammy Phillips talks about a man who had a heart attack and died in the bar one evening. The police arrived and ran a check on the man, discovered that there was a warrant for his arrest, and proceeded to handcuff the corpse to the pool table.

> **☛Visiting the Time Out Lounge:** The neon lights that announce your arrival at the Time Out are throwbacks to a time when neon was king in Anchorage. The bar has a huge dance floor and a big room downstairs that has seen its share of parties, wakes, and poker tournaments.

Flight Deck Bar
832 International Airport Road, Anchorage
(907) 563-6156

License Issued: August 4, 1971, to Fred Pogue Brothers and Sons Enterprises Inc.
Amenities: Pool tables, darts, corn hole, TVs, food occasional live music
Find them Online: Facebook

History and Notoriety: Fred, Loren, and Gerald Pogue were born and raised in St. Louis, Missouri, before moving to Alaska. In 1969, they owned a liquor store at this location before obtaining a license for a bar and hotel, which they named the Flight Deck. This was (and is) a convenient place for people to have a drink before heading to the airport. For a time, the brothers also owned The Pines bar, which closed in 1993. They sold the Flight Deck to John Widmer in 1974. Widmer died four years later at the young age of 46, but the Widmer family owned the bar until 1991, when they sold to the Ivory Manufacturing Corporation. The restaurant was added that same year.

The bar has sponsored softball teams for many years, known as the "Flight Deckers."

In 2009, a man with a long criminal record was arrested at the Flight Deck and charged with the murder of a local woman. According to the bartenders, who recognized him from photos on TV and called police, the man was a regular who enjoyed drinking Miller Genuine Draft, shooting pool and dancing by himself.

> ☛**Visiting the Flight Deck:** This bar is known for its huge pizzas, which are long on sauce and quality ingredients. The interior is dated but comfortable, and the bartenders and regular patrons are very friendly.

Great Alaskan Bush Company
(a.k.a. Bush Company, a.k.a. BC)
631 East International Airport Road, Anchorage
(907) 561-2609

License Issued: July 12, 1984, to Edna Cox and John Cox
Amenities: Live adult entertainment, gift shop, pool tables
Find them Online: https://www.akbushcompany.com/; Facebook

History and Notoriety: The Great Alaskan Bush Company is the only strip bar included in this book. There are other strip bars in Alaska, but the Bush Company is in a class by itself, and one of the most famous bars in Alaska. The International Airport Road location was originally Bush Company II but became the one and only when the older Bush Company on Fifth Avenue downtown closed in 1989 due to plumbing and other problems.

Both bars were among of the last bars in Alaska where the "B-Girl" practices of encouraging men to buy drinks were kept alive. The so-called "champagne hustle" works very well when a scantily clad dancer asks a patron to buy a one-hundred-dollar bottle under the assumption that she will be imbibing as well. The reality was that the girls would pour their portions out on the floor when the customers weren't looking. Because of this, the Bush Company on Fifth Avenue eventually acquired an awful, fermented smell. When Bush Company II was built, drain holes were drilled in the floors of all the booths. After several liquor license suspensions, both bars ended the B-Girl practice.

Edna Cox was a shrewd businesswoman and a terrific hostess. She and her son John "Jack" turned over control of the bar to Jack's wife Vicki in 1990. Managing strip clubs is a job usually done by men, but Vicki, a beautiful blond with a heart of gold, excelled at it. Having a woman manager attracted a lot of talent over the years, and she treated all the girls like family. She passed away in 2011.

The Bush Company is still owned by the Cox family.

Anchorage is an international air crossroads, and the Bush Company is located just ten minutes from the airport. This allows men from all over the world to visit the bar, even if they're only in town for a few hours. The bar is popular with servicemen and has been the scene of a countless number of bachelor parties. While the patrons are mostly male, couples are made to feel welcome also.

☛**Visiting the Great Alaskan Bush Company**: The main stage is the prominent feature and can be seen clearly from almost anywhere in the bar. The Bush Company has always hired an incredible variety of women, and many are from Alaska. These ladies are very friendly and rarely pushy, and the drinks are reasonably priced. Consider trying a Bushwhacker cocktail. FYI – table dances are twenty dollars.

Eddie's Sports Bar
6300 Old Seward Highway, Anchorage
(907) 563-3970

License Issued: June 14, 1994, to Eddie James (Rockdance Inc.)
Amenities: Pool tables, darts, shuffleboard, TVs, food, occasional live entertainment
Find them Online: Facebook

History and Notoriety: Edward "Eddie" James (real name Nadime Ganam) was born in Damascus, Syria, in 1935. His family emigrated to New York in 1944. As a young man, James shined shoes and served in the US Marine Corps. In Las Vegas, he met and married a girl from Alaska and moved to Anchorage in 1965.

Starting in 1971, he opened a series of bars in Anchorage, beginning with Eddie's Sandbox, followed by The Waterhole (1972), Eddie's Hayloft (1976), Temporary Affair (1980), Eddie's (1980), Hacienda (1981), Ambassador (1985), and the Hacienda II (1986). By 1987, all these bars had closed. However, James still owned or had a partial interest in other Anchorage bars such as the Panhandle, Polar, and JJ's Lounge.

In 1975, James married Patricia "Patsy" from Oklahoma. In 1994, he opened a sports bar on Old Seward Hwy. On the liquor license application, he crossed out "Temporary Affair" and hand wrote "Eddie's Sports Bar." Joining him in the venture were Patsy, brother Mike, son Martin, and daughter Sharolyn. TVs were placed around the bar showing a variety of sports, but mostly football. The bar's basement became a meeting place for groups, such as fans of the Minnesota Vikings. The basement would soon have a bar, sound system, dance floor, and stage. Eddie's "Comedy Cellar" was a good place to see comedians in the late 1990s. In 2013, the backyard of Eddie's was where the first Backyard Country Barbecue was held, with lots of food and live country music.

In 2015, James sold the bar to his granddaughter Darolyn Raskin and Tim Dudley. He spent much of his retirement golfing, bowling, and playing poker. James passed away in 2020 and is buried in the National Cemetery at Fort Richardson.

> ☛**Visiting Eddie's Sports Bar**: The gray square building with the red roof is a place where you can eat breakfast, lunch, or dinner and watch your favorite game. Eddie's is the place to be after Rodeo Alaska.

Eddie James (1935 – 2020). Photo courtesy of Darolyn Raskin

Al's Alaskan Inn
7830 Old Seward Highway, Anchorage
(907) 344-6223

License Name Change Issued: August 31, 1976, to Allen I. Choy

Amenities: Pool tables, darts, shuffle boards, TVs, occasional live music, food

Find them Online: Facebook

History and Notoriety: Allen "Big Al" Choy was born in Hawaii in 1928. He moved to Alaska in 1956 and opened the Candle Inn at this location in 1961. After the 1964 earthquake, he added a bar and barbershop. Choy changed the name to Al's Alaskan Inn in 1976. Allen Jr. was born in 1966 and eventually began running the business with his father. In 1999 Big Al transferred ownership to Al Jr. Although he'd been raised on the motto "our customers are our family," Al Jr. made the decision to leave the comfort zone of customers he had inherited from his father and pursue a younger crowd as well as tourists. In 2002, Al Jr. spent over a million dollars and added several theme bars inside the Alaskan Inn. Big Al passed away in 2006.

Also in 2006, Al Jr. purchased a 58-foot double-decker Alaska Railroad car with the intention of hoisting it to the building's second story to expand the bar. Two years later, the City of Anchorage denied his request and ordered him to remove the railroad car. In an act of defiance, Al Jr. put an iron sculpture of a 7-foot locomotive on top of a twenty-foot-tall tripod. He calls it the "Soul Train."

In 2022, a man was shot and killed by another man on the dance floor at Al's. The shooter was arrested and charged with first and second-degree murder.

> **☛Visiting Al's Alaskan Inn**: Al's is a U-shaped two-story building that is packed with a wide variety of things you can do, see and eat. Note the headless Fat Albert holding the keg on the patio. Al Jr. was warned that he couldn't use the cartoon character without permission, hence the missing head.

Allen Choy Jr. and Sr. Photo courtesy of Allen Choy Jr

JJ's Lounge
624 Muldoon, Anchorage
(907) 338-9855

License issued: November 20, 1972, to Joe Kinnebrew and James Link
Amenities: Pool, darts, horseshoes, TVs.
Find Them Online: Facebook

History and Notoriety: Joe Kinnebrew was born in Arizona and James "Jim" Link was born in Wisconsin. Both men joined the Air Force and became electricians. Jim moved to Alaska in 1959 and Joe by 1970. Their paths crossed and they decided to go into business together. Joe convinced Jim that Anchorage needed a neighborhood bar where people could warm up, relax and swap stories. They chose the name "JJ" from the first letter of their first names. JJ's Lounge opened in December of 1972, and in 1976 they brought Jim's wife Elaine on board to serve as Secretary/Treasurer. Joe was frequently at JJ's while Jim considered himself a "silent partner." Joe loved anything that was Irish, especially St. Patricks' Day, hence the shamrocks on the building sign. Joe also made sure that the bathrooms at JJ's were immaculate.

Joe and Jim sold JJs in 1986 and the new owner changed the name of the bar to the Fox's Den. Joe and Jim bought it back in 1989 and restored the JJ's name. In 1992 they sold the bar to Eddie and Patsy James (see Eddie's Sports Bar) and their partners Jerry and Sheilah Buffington. The name of the bar has remained JJ's ever since, sometimes with the additional words Muldoon Sports Center or Sports Lounge. Joe and his wife Diana moved to Washington state where Joe passed away in 2014.

In October of 2011, JJs was unfortunately the scene of a late-night argument that resulted in gunfire. Two men were killed, one of them just outside the entrance to the bar, and the other in the southbound lane of Muldoon Road. Two other people, both unarmed and one a woman, were also shot but only wounded. One man was charged with murder, the other man with murder and with attempted murder.

> **Visiting JJ's Lounge:** This is still a neighborhood bar and a great place to shoot pool and throw darts. There's also horseshoe pits in the backyard and barbecues during the summer months. St. Patrick's Day is always observed at JJ's.

Joe Kinnebrew in a catholic priest costume at JJ's. Photo courtesy of Diana Kinnebrew

The Cabin Tavern
264 Muldoon Road, Anchorage
(907) 338-9905

License Issued: September 17, 1981, to Daniel Zivanich and Edward DeSapio
Amenities: Pool tables, darts, TVs, occasional live music
Find them Online: Facebook

History and Notoriety: The Cabin Tavern has its roots in a bar known as Swifty's Club 13 which opened in this building at this location in 1956. In 1974, the bar was sold to Martin, Andrew, and Jane Slisco who changed the name to The Roadhouse. The Slisco' sold the bar to Daniel Zivanich and Edward DeSapio in 1981, who changed the name to The Cabin Tavern.

According to an article by *Anchorage Daily News* reporter Julia O'Malley, "Danny" Zivanich and "Tiny" DeSapio met in 1971 just after Tiny moved to Anchorage from Honolulu, where he had been a knife and fire dancer in the Don Ho Show. Zivanich first saw DeSapio at the Chef's Inn in Anchorage (closed in 2014) where Zivanich was tending bar. DeSapio, who was in for a drink, tried to help him break up a bar fight. Zivanich, who is five foot eight inches, looked up at DeSapio, who stood six foot eight inches and said thanks but "you'll make things much worse."

The two became fast friends even though they had opposite personalities. DeSapio loved a good crowd, but he had rules for the Cabin Tavern. Patrons should be polite and refrain from using four-letter words, and anyone who carried out the trash got a drink on the house. DeSapio passed away from cancer in 2010, and his ashes were spread over the roof of the Cabin Tavern.

The Cabin Tavern is reportedly haunted, with spirits making their presence known via the usual acts of mischief (items falling over by themselves, unexplained noises etc.)

> **☛Visiting The Cabin Tavern:** The building is a genuine log cabin complete with wooden tables and a beautiful, polished wood bar. Note the grass on the sod roof, the fireplace and adjacent take-one-leave-one bookshelf, and the Alaskan animal paintings. Most drinks are served in Mason jar glasses. Leave a tip in the hanging spittoon.

NOTORIOUS BARS OF SOUTHCENTRAL ALASKA 95

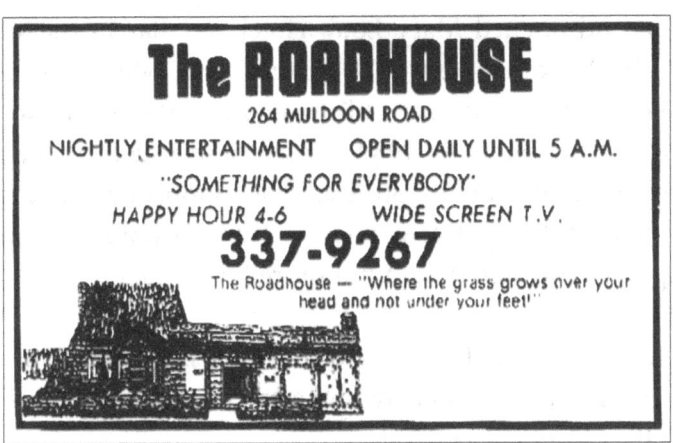

From the Anchorage Telephone Directory – 1979.

Brown Bear Saloon
28065 (Mile 103) Seward Highway, Indian
(907) 653-7000

License Name Change Issued: November 1989 to Mary Lou Redmond
Amenities: Pool table, darts, TVs, food. occasional live music
Find them Online: http://www.brownbearalaska.com/; Facebook

History and Notoriety: Mary Lou Redmond, born in Iowa, moved to Alaska in 1952 when she was 18. She had an uncle named Jim Toman who was known as "Diamond Jim." Toman owned Diamond Jim's, a bar in the town of Portage at the head of Turnagain Arm. Toman died in 1956, and Redmond inherited the bar. The 1964 earthquake destroyed Portage and the bar. The federal government relocated the business, including a large neon sign, to Indian, some twenty-five miles northwest of Portage. This sign has become a landmark in the community.

Redmond opened Mary Lou's Hotel and Bar in the summer of 1984 in the lot adjacent to Diamond Jim's, which had become just a liquor store. She changed the name of the hotel and bar to the Brown Bear Saloon in 1989 and sold it in 1996. She then operated Diamond Jim's Liquor Store and Gift Shop, and after a lengthy battle with the Alaska Department of Transportation, was allowed to keep the neon sign. Redmond retired in 2019 and passed away in 2022.

In June 2013, the first "Brown Bear Music Festival" was held. The event featured eight bands and a barbecue. It is now called the Brown Bear Summer Festival.

☛**Visiting the Brown Bear Saloon**: The Brown Bear is a great place to hang out after skiing at Alyeska, or, when you need a break from fighting the summer traffic. If you become a little too relaxed, you can stay right there, order a hamburger, and rent a hotel room or cabin.

Mary Lou Redmond (1934 – 2022) and the neon sign.
Loren Holmes / Anchorage Daily News archive – *July 23, 2012*

Anchor Inn
(a.k.a. Overview Lounge)
Corner of Whittier Street and Depot Road, Whittier
(907) 472-2354

License Issued: August 24, 1979, to Robert and Fei Harding
Amenities: TVs, food, occasional live music
Find them Online: http://www.anchorinnwhittier.com

History and Notoriety: The building that houses the Anchor Inn was built in 1943 and is the oldest building in Whittier. During the 1940s and '50s, the town was an active US Army facility, and the building housed the Alaska Communication System. The Army left Whittier in 1960, but a few people decided to stay. The Harding's converted the building into a hotel and bar and sold it to Chou and YenWen Shen in 1982. The Anchor is now a multi-purpose two-building facility, which for many years included the only bar in Whittier open year-round.

The Anchor Inn and its neighbor, the Sportsman's Inn have, on occasion, been forced to cater to more than just than the town residents and summer tourists. In 1989, the oil tanker *Exxon Valdez* spilled eleven million gallons of crude oil into Prince William Sound. Hundreds of workers descended on the town, filling both bars to capacity for weeks. In 1995, a fire broke out on the *Regent Star* cruise ship forcing the evacuation of 850 passengers. The crew of 450 spent a week in Whittier while the ship was being repaired. The Anchor Inn provided a refuge for the crew, including the ships band, which would play all night at the bar.

Prior to 2000, the only way to get to Whittier from the Seward Highway was by taking a shuttle train from Portage. Being in Whittier was sometimes like being in prison, with almost no options for escape if the notion occurred to you. In 1998, a man who had been drinking at the Anchor Inn decided that he just had to get out of Whittier. He got into his truck and drove on the railroad tracks towards Portage. He made it through the first tunnel but got stuck leaving the tracks, after which he was soon arrested.

☛**Visiting the Anchor Inn:** The main bar at the Anchor Inn, named the "Overview Lounge," is located on the third floor and has a good view of Passage Canal. A smaller bar is on the second floor in the restaurant. Be sure to look at the museum just down the hall in the adjacent two-story building. Independence Day is one of the most celebrated days in Whittier and is a good time to be at the Anchor Inn.

Sportsman's Inn
Depot Road, Whittier
(907) 472-2354

License Name Change Issued: 1966 to Prince William Sound Development Co. (Rodger Franck, Lawrence Palmer, and Ray Grundhauser

Amenities: Pool tables, darts, shuffleboard, corn hole, occasional live music, food

Find them Online: Facebook

History and Notoriety: The row of condominiums now known as Whittier Manor was built in the early 1950s to house Army personnel with families. When the Army left Whittier in 1960, the condos sat idle until a group of developers decided to renovate the building into a resort. They named it the Chenaga Inn after the local village that had been destroyed by the 1964 earthquake. The resort opened that summer and included a cafeteria, dining room and rustic style lounge. Two years later the name was changed to the Sportsman's Inn.

Longtime resident Kay Shepard described the Whittier social scene of the early 1970s in a 1986 article in the *Anchorage Daily News*: "Fifteen years ago they used to get together at the Sportsman's Inn. They'd dance and drink strawberry punch, spiked of course. You might notice a few bullet holes in the walls there. People used to get a little angry about things. Not so much anymore. We have our factions, but things are more settled. Now we've got two inns, the Anchor and the Sportsman's. Both have parties. Sometimes they have potlucks. Sometimes there's a band. It can be a lot of fun. You ought to come down."

Rawson and Irma Knight took over in 1974 and took on partners John and Audrey Whedbee in 1975. Together they managed the hotel, restaurant, bar, general store, theatre, and gift shop until 1991. After two more sets of owners, Chou and YenWen Shen (who also own the Anchor Inn) bought the Sportsman's in 1996.

☛**Visiting the Sportsman's Inn**: The vertical letters that spelled out Sportsman's Inn, which used to run down the length of the awning over the stairs leading up to the bar, blew off years ago and were never replaced. This is the most rustic of the two bars in Whittier, and more frequented by the locals.

Tony's Bar (Seward)
135 Fourth Avenue, Seward
(907) 224-3045

License Name Change Issued: 1945 to Tony Parich
Amenities: Pool table, TVs, food, occasional live music, liquor store
Find them Online: Facebook

History and Notoriety: Tony Parich was born in 1879 in Dalmatia, Austria. He moved to the U.S. in 1907 and was a soldier in World War I. Parich and his brother Sam Romack moved to Seward from Portland, Oregon in 1922. During prohibition, both men were making and selling moonshine. By 1933, Parich owned the Seward Hotel and Bar and the Spokane Rooms and Bar. People staying at the Spokane Rooms began referring to the bar as "Tony's" and the name became official in 1945. Parich had a habit of greeting everyone with "Good Morning" regardless of what time of day it was. He passed away in December 1947, and his death and funeral made front page news in Seward. Sam Romack took over management of the bar.

According to Seward historian Mary J. Barry, Romack started the tradition of Tony's celebrating St. Patrick's Day with a free smorgasbord, which included ham, turkey, and his home-made sauerkraut, made from a 200-year-old secret family recipe. Romack continued to operate the bar even after he lost his left leg to diabetes. When Romack died in 1974, his nephew Johan Banic took over Tony's and continued the tradition of free buffets for special occasions. The Banic family sold the bar to the Schroder family, the current owners.

➥**Visiting Tony's Bar:** This historic bar is the place to be when you want to relax, enjoy a drink, and listen to a local musician. Food is served here during the holidays.

From Lou Jacobin's Guide to Alaska and the Yukon – 1954.

Flamingo Lounge
(a.k.a. Thorns, a.k.a. Showcase)
208 Fourth Avenue, Seward
(907) 599-0133

License Issued: October 20, 1971, to Louis Eugene "Gene" Thorn
Amenities: TVs, restaurant
Find them Online: https://flamingoalaska.com/; Facebook

History and Notoriety: The Flamingo has its roots in a bar known as Gil's Lounge which was in the Palace Café Building in 1947 and moved to this location in 1950. Harley "Hal" and Clair Gilfilin owned Gil's until 1962 when they sold it to Dorothy Johnson, who hired Louis "Gene" Thorn as Manager. The building was damaged by a fire in January 1971, but by October, Thorn and his wife Pat had bought, rebuilt, refurbished, and renamed the bar Thorn's Showcase.

Many people associate the bar with the 1960s era bubble-letter neon sign out front, the dimly lit interior, the red chairs-on-rollers, and Alaska's largest collection of Jim Beam bottles and decanters. And of course, the Bucket of Butt, which is a basket of deep-fried halibut.

Pat Thorn passed away in 2017 and Gene followed in 2020. In 2022 the bar was bought by Seward locals Matt Cope and his wife Kelly Ann Cavaretta. Cope and Cavaretta appreciate the history of this bar and have decided to keep most of the exterior and interior features. The Thorn family requested that the name of the bar be changed, and the new owners chose the Flamingo Lounge, in honor of an old Seward bar that opened in 1953 and was closed by 1983.

☛Visiting the Flamingo Lounge: The new owners have given this bar a serious upgrade in the way of cocktails and food. There's a White Russian cocktail named after Gene Thorn, and a Tomahawk Steak is available too. Independence Day is a popular time to visit the Flamingo, as well as Thanksgiving and Christmas.

Yukon Bar
(a.k.a. The Kon)
201 Fourth Avenue, Seward
(907) 224-3063

License Issued: November 7, 1949, to Vance and Amelia Hitt
Amenities: Pool table, occasional live music
Find them Online: Facebook

History and Notoriety: In 1903, Don Carlos Brownell Sr. bought the lot for one thousand dollars, on which the Yukon Bar is now located and built the D.C. Brownell Hardware Store. This was the first lot to be sold in the new railroad town of Seward. Brownwell died in 1915, and the hardware store closed. The building was destroyed by fire and was rebuilt, and by 1947 was the home of Novick's Cocktail Bar. In 1949, William Novick sold the bar to Vance and Amelia "Amy" Hitt, who changed the name to the Yukon Bar. Vance, from West Virginia, had lived in Seward since 1934. He and his wife Amy, born in Fairbanks, owned several other businesses in town, as well as Vance's Bar in Nenana. Vance Hitt sold the bar to Faye Culbertson in 1951 but owned the building until his death in 1979.

The early Yukon Bar used running water to keep their beer "teeth chilling" cold, supplied from the Hoben & Davis Water Co. directly across the street. The only drawback was that the labels would come loose from the bottles, and if the bartender was busy, you might not know what kind of beer was served.

In his book *Looking for Alaska*, author Peter Jenkins titled a chapter "Hobo Night" which in part described a performance of Hobo Jim at the Yukon Bar. Jim Varsos (a.k.a. Hobo Jim) was a guitar playing song writer, who is best known for writing "The Iditarod Song." His many performances at the Yukon Bar (and throughout Alaska) were extremely entertaining, particularly if he decided to indulge in some shots of tequila. Varsos passed away from cancer in 2021.

Many people associate the Yukon Bar with the Mount Marathon Race, held every year on Independence Day. The race began in 1915 when someone claimed that it was impossible to climb the mountain and return to town in less than an hour. Many people have accomplished that very feat over the years. The finish line for the race is directly in front of the Yukon, which results in many sweaty and occasionally bloody racers having beers in the bar.

☛**Visiting the Yukon Bar:** The Yukon is the bar in Seward most likely to have live music, even during the winter months. Independence Day is the most popular time to be at the Yukon (standing room only, assuming you can get in the door). Halloween is also quite popular.

The Yukon Bar in the 1950s.
Vern Brickley Collection; Anchorage Museum, B1998.014.1.2022

Maverick Saloon
(a.k.a. The Mav)
44698 Sterling Highway, Soldotna
(907) 260-5685

License Name Change Issued: 1972 to Lawrence and Florence Lancashire and Jack Rose
Amenities: Pool tables, TVs, food, occasional live music
Find them Online: Facebook

History and Notoriety: The Ace of Clubs bar was located here from 1960 – 1971. Lawrence "Larry" and Florence "Rusty" Lancashire moved to Alaska from the Midwest in 1948 and owned

Larry's Club in Kenai (1964 – 1996). The Lancashires bought the Ace of Clubs in 1971 and changed its name to Rod's Club. They took on Jack Rose, from Wyoming, as a partner the following year and changed the name to the Maverick Club. The trio sold the Maverick in 1984, but the Lancashires bought it back again in 1997. Larry passed away that same year and Rusty sold the bar in 1998. The new owners changed the name to the Maverick Saloon.

The word maverick is defined as an independent individual who does not go along with a party or group. Maverick has been used to describe people who live in the southern states, and also Alaskans. Check out the Confederate and Alaskan flags encased side-by-side with the motto "Maverick Saloon – Where the North and South meet."

The bar is popular with fishermen, bikers, and equestrians. The Soldotna Rodeo Grounds are less than 5 minutes away. Once after a rodeo, a competitor rode his horse into the bar and asked for a shot, which he promptly drank while still in the saddle.

In 2012 the bar acquired two historical items from the now closed Clam Shell Lodge bar in Clam Gulch: a piano and a huge razor clam in a jar. The razor clam must be seen to be believed.

☞Visiting the Maverick Saloon: The Maverick operates on a schedule from eight o'clock in the morning to five o'clock in the morning every single day of the year. A Kenai Peninsula bar that is closed for only 3 hours a day is unique. All the usual celebratory days are observed here, with Halloween and New Years Eve being particularly festive.

4 Royle Parkers
(a.k.a. Parker's)
36185 Kenai Spur Highway, Soldotna
(907) 262-4670

License Name Change Issued: 1958 to Royle and Betty Parker
Amenities: Pool tables, TVs, food, occasional live music
Find them Online: Facebook

History and Notoriety: Royle Parker was born in Salt Lake City, Utah, in 1917. Betty "Mickey" Peterson was born in McGill, Nevada, in 1927. They married in 1946 and moved to Anchorage in 1948. By 1950, they had a son, Royle Jr., and a daughter, Susie. In 1952, the Parker's moved to Kenai, where Mickey found work at the newly opened Rainbow Bar and Cafe. In 1955, they opened a café in an area between Kenai and Soldotna known as Ironsville, now called Ridgeway. In 1956, Mickey got a liquor license for the café, issued in her name.

In 1957, production of oil and gas in the Swanson River area north of Kenai created jobs and attracted a large influx of people. In 1958, the Parker's changed the name of their cafe to 4 Royle Parkers, 4 reflecting the four members of their family. A dining room was added adjacent to the bar, which became known as the "Board Room" and was the scene of many meetings between oil company officials. It was also where locals celebrated holidays and anniversaries. The cocktail lounge was dubbed "The Office."

By 1960, 4 Royle Parkers had added a gas station, motel, barber shop, and liquor store. The Parker's sponsored local events, such as Soldotna "Progress Day" parades, sled dog races, and ball games at "Parker's Field" behind their complex.

Tragically, Royle Sr. disappeared after his boat capsized on the Copper River near Lake Iliamna in 1969. Mickey married Harry

Petroulias in 1971, retired in 1985, and sold the bar to Taek and Hee Lee. Mickey passed away in 1986.

Taek and Hee were both born in South Korea. They married and moved to Alaska in 1983, and had a son, Edward "Eddie" in 1991. Taek passed away in 2019, and Parkers is now owned by Hee and Eddie.

☛**Visiting 4 Royle Parkers**: It is a tribute to the Parker family that the Lee family is still using the 4 Royle Parkers name for this bar. While the gas station and barber are gone, you can still eat and drink in this very well-kept historic building. Note the old drill bits from the oil field that surround the building like parking meters, and the old piano. Live music can be found here on the weekends.

Royle Parker Sr. behind the bar at 4 Royle Parkers, June 30, 1960. Property of Kenai Peninsula College. KPC-PC-0593

The Bow
(a.k.a. Rainbow Bar)
502 South Main Street, Kenai
(907) 283-3385

License Issued: 1953 to Tony and Eyvhon Bordenelli
Amenities: Pool tables, TVs, food, occasional live music
Find them Online: Facebook (thebowbar)

History and Notoriety: The Rainbow Bar has been a Kenai institution for many years and is truly a classic Alaskan bar. When it first opened, it was in conjunction with a café. The original building, which was much smaller, has been replaced but the location has remained the same.

Beginning in 1967 and lasting through the 1980s, the Rainbow was one-third of the "Devils Triangle" bar crawl route, the other two bars being The Rig and The Casino. All three bars were within easy walking distance of each other (the Casino was across the street). The Rig closed in 1987 and the Casino in 2018.

Ownership of the Rainbow has changed hands frequently over the years. Harry and Barbara Axson held onto it the longest, buying the bar in 1975 and selling it twenty years later.

So many people refer to the bar as simply "the Bow" that the owners have changed the name. The current moniker reflects a bow used to shoot arrows.

☞**Visiting The Bow:** Of the many Alaska bars that celebrate Halloween, the party that occurs here is perhaps one of the most elaborate. Preparations begin a month in advance and always include an incredible number of cobwebs. Some years, an entire graveyard has been constructed. Note that the dance floor at the Bow has a pole at one corner, which has seen its share of spontaneous pole dances.

From Lou Jacobin's Guide to Alaska and the Yukon – 1954.

Kenai Joe's Taphouse
(a.k.a. Kenai Joe's)
800 Cook Avenue, Kenai
(907) 283-5637

License Issued: 1947 to John Consiel Sr.
Amenities: Pool table, darts, corn hole, TVs, food, occasional live music
Find them Online: Facebook

History and Notoriety: John "Kenai Joe" Consiel Sr. was born in Poland in 1896. He made his way to Alaska via New York, Detroit, and Prince Rupert, arriving in the new town of Anchorage in 1915 and then Kenai in 1917. He built "Keen Eye Joe's Roadhouse" adjacent to the Kenai River, receiving title to the property in 1934. In 1935, he built the building that currently houses the bar and obtained a retail liquor license. By 1947, he had a roadhouse license. That same year, he married Elsie, and together they managed the bar, a hotel, and raised two sons. Kenai Joe passed away in 1970, though Elsie was a partner in the bar until 1989, when Roy Howard took over.

In 2019, the Kenai River Brewing Company bought Kenai Joe's and added the word 'Taphouse' to the name, and craft cocktails to the list of drinks available.

"To Joe's We Goes" is still a popular sentiment for the folks who live in this area. The bar is large, with plenty of room to mingle, dance, play games, and celebrate being at a truly historic Alaska institution.

☛Visiting Kenai Joe's: This is a not-to-be-missed bar on the Kenai Peninsula. The new owners have added a deck which is a great place to hang out. Come on a weekend when there is a live band and plan to stay for a while.

"Kenai Joe" Consiel behind his bar – 1947.
Property of Kenai Peninsula College, KPC-PC-0689

Vagabond Inn
38515 Kalifornsky Beach Road, Kenai
(907) 283-9211

License Issued: 1971 to Barney and Charlotte Kyzer
Amenities: Pool table, TVs, occasional live music, liquor store
Find them Online: Facebook

History and Notoriety: Barney and Charlotte Kyzer opened the Vagabond in 1966 as just a liquor store but expanded the business into a bar in 1971. They added James and Kathleen Barr as partners in 1974 and sold the Vagabond to the Barrs in 1978.

Be looking for the Vagabond sign which sits atop a 60' pole at the driveway to the bar. The pole is taller than the trees surrounding it. The moniker of the Vagabond Bar is a fishing vessel, and the bar exhibits a nautical theme.

For the record: the final striptease of Eadie Sutton Henderson, owner of the notorious Last Frontier Club in Kenai (closed in 1999) was at the Vagabond Inn on December 11, 1999, at the age of 73. She lost her battle with cancer the following month after a twenty-six-year struggle.

☛**Visiting the Vagabond Inn:** This is a beautiful, well-kept neighborhood establishment that looks like a residence when first seen.

The Place
53791 Sparrow Lane, Kenai
(907) 283-7034

License Name Change Issued: December 2, 1975, to Ray and Thelma Goudreau and Thomas Tomdle.
Amenities: Pool tables, darts, TVs, food, occasional live entertainment
Find them Online: Facebook (theplacemotelbar)

History and Notoriety: In 1967, the motel at this location was called The Place, and the attached bar and café were called The Hard Hat. Workers from the nearby Swanson River oil and gas field were the primary customers. Owners Ray and Thelma Goudreau took on Thomas Tomdle as a partner in 1973 and changed the name of the bar to The Place in 1975. In 1979, The Place was sold to Donald Clark and Donald Aase.

Clark grew up in the Homer area and was a WWII fighter pilot nicknamed the "Alaska Kid." After the war, he became a stunt pilot and was in the 1970 film *Tora! Tora! Tora!* where he crash-lands a plane on one wheel.

Aase grew up in Owatonna, Minnesota and graduated from

high school in 1946. He moved to Kenai and invested in real estate. His sister Lorna married Rodney Young, and their son John was born in 1951 in Owatonna. John graduated from high school in 1969, got married in 1970, became a father, and divorced in 1974. In 1976, he moved to Alaska to work as an Insulator on the Alaska Pipeline. It was during this time he got the nickname "Grizz." At some point Grizz visited his Uncle Donald, got a close look at The Place, and bought the bar from Donald Clark in 1987. Soon, bear statues, pelts, and even a fully taxidermized grizzly adorned the bar. During the 1980s, the city of Kenai called itself the "Oil Capital of Alaska" and oil field workers continued to be frequent customers at The Place.

In 2009, Wee Man (real name Jason Acuna) from the *Jackass* movies, visited The Place. The 4'6" tall actor signed an autograph on the torso of one local young man. "I love it here" he said of his time in Alaska.

Grizz suffered from Lou Gehrig's disease and passed away in 2015. His son Jason moved to Kenai from Minnesota to keep The Place going until he could sell it. Grant and Rosanna Gratrix bought the bar in 2017. Grant grew up in Alaska and Rosanna is originally from the Philippines.

☛**Visiting The Place:** While most of the bear mementos are gone, this is a fun bar that is popular with dart throwers. Be sure to take the short walk outside to "The Table" which has a commanding view of Cook Inlet and the Iliamna Volcano.

Forelands Bar
54728 Industrial Ave (Mile 21 Kenai Spur Hwy), Nikiski
(907) 776-5833

License Issued: June 8, 1960, to Leonard and Hazel Holt
Amenities: Pool table, TVs, occasional live music, liquor store
Find them Online: Facebook

History and Notoriety: The Forelands Bar was born in the early days of the Kenai oil boom. The name refers to the nearby east and west forelands, points of land that form a narrowing of Cook Inlet. The Grand Opening of the bar was on May 27, 1961, and featured free pizza "made from a secret old Indian recipe by Hazel Holt."

The bar was first located at Mile 12 of the North Road (now the Kenai Spur Hwy.) and moved to its current location in 1972. The spelling has varied from Forelands to Fourlands to 4 Lands, and from 1984 – 1986 it was known as the Nikiski House. The original sign, spelled Fourlands, was removed when the Kenai Spur Highway was widened.

Beginning in 1982, a local artist named John Wilkes began decorating the wooden serving bar and the tables with a wood burner. The etchings represent Alaska themes and most of them are very well done.

Eadie Sutton Henderson, the renowned owner of Eadie's Last Frontier Club in Kenai (closed in 1999) did a strip tease dance at the Forelands in 1999. Even though she was in her 70's, she still had a beautiful body and danced very gracefully. Eadie still retained a certain dignity and advised a local girl who also danced that evening to "don't show no rabbit."

☛**Visiting the Forelands Bar:** The Forelands throws an "MMM Party" on a weekend in May that celebrates May Day, Mother's Day, and Memorial Day. Food is served on Halloween and New Years Eve.

From Alaska Highway Sketches by Connie Silver – 1962.

Hunger Hut Bar
(a.k.a. The Hut)
51815 Kenai Spur Hwy, Nikiski
(907) 776-5853

License Issued: 1966 to Wilfred F. Hatcher and Frank and Elsie Moore
Amenities: Pool table, darts, TVs, food, occasional live music, liquor store
Find them Online: Facebook

History and Notoriety: The Hunger Hut began as a restaurant, but because its customers were mostly oil field workers and fishermen (primarily a drinking crowd) a liquor license was soon obtained. Frank and Elsie Moore took control of the bar in 1968. Thelma McConnell became a partner in 1972, and the owner in 1986. She passed away in 1993, and her daughter, Linda Superman, and son, Timothy Stolz inherited the bar. Stolz passed away in 2004 and Superman became the owner.

The Hut is famous for being the home of the "Pussy Posse." The Pussy Posse was founded by the local Old Timers Club and during the early 1970s, traveled via their "Big Blue Bitch Bus" to bars and lodges on the Kenai Peninsula to sing, perform skits, and tell bawdy jokes. The money raised went to buy toys, bikes, skis, and the like for kids that lived in Nikiski. Superman shared with me a photo album full of photos of the Pussy Posse in a vast variety of costumes. The performances eventually became overcrowded with out-of-towners who cared more about partying than helping the cause.

In the book *Last Call!* Superman told author Richard Robinson some great stories about the Pussy Posse which included as one of their members a six-foot seven inch, four-hundred-pound man named "Big John" who dressed like a baby in a diaper (!). Also interviewed was Hut bartender Peggy Freed, who told an incredible story of a man who was arrested at the bar and taken to jail. The man returned to the bar an hour later, explaining that he told the cops to "put it on my tab."

> **☛Visiting the Hunger Hut Bar:** The Hut is open 365 days a year. In the tradition of the Pussy Posse, Halloween is celebrated with a costume contest. Thanksgiving and Christmas are also good times to visit.

Decanter Inn
Mile 107 Sterling Highway, Kasilof
(907) 262-5917

License Issued: March 27, 1966, to Tony and Mary Correia
Amenities: Pool table, food, occasional live music
Find them Online: Facebook

History and Notoriety: Antone Joao "Tony J" Correia, a WWII vet originally from California, came to Anchorage in 1952 and homesteaded in this area in 1954. In 1966, Tony J and Mary Correia bought the liquor license for Lola's Bar and changed the name to The Decanter, referencing an ornamental glass bottle used for serving wine. They also purchased the adjacent property which included two lakes. Tony J was a skilled welder, and in 1967, he welded a large capital letter "T" marking the new road to Tustumena Lake. The distinctive "T" is still at Mile 111 of the Sterling Highway out in front of the Tustumena Lodge. Tony J also started the Decanter tradition of "ice racing" cars and snowmobiles on the frozen lakes adjacent to the bar.

The Correias divorced in 1979, and the bar was sold in 1984. The establishment was known as the Black Eagle Saloon until 1988, when brothers Terry and Bud Wallace bought the bar and changed the name to the Decanter Inn. Other spellings are DeCanter and De Canter.

From 1984 to 1993, the Tustumena 200 Sled Dog Race began and ended at the Decanter. The two-hundred-mile course crossed Tustumena Lake and continued south to Homer, where the mushers turned around and came back to the Decanter. The most recent Tustumena 200 started and ended in Ninilchik.

These days, the Decanter is known for ice racing and for music festivals held during the summer months.

☞**Visiting the Decanter Inn:** The Fisherman's Ball in August features bands, Cajun food, and craft vendors. Also check out the Hippie Olympics in October.

From The Cheechako News – December 6, 1978.

Tustumena Lodge
(a.k.a. The Big T)
58840 (Mile 111) Sterling Highway, Kasilof
(907) 260-3122

License Issued: March 7, 1991, to John Cook
Amenities: Pool tables, TVs, food, occasional live music
Find them Online: Facebook

History and Notoriety: From 1930 – 1948, there was a Tustumena Lodge in this area, owned by Mr. and Mrs. Ernest W. Hull, which catered to big game hunters during the summer months. The Sterling Highway was completed from Soldotna to Homer in 1950, and the Kasilof area was opened to homesteading in 1955. In 1976, Nikola Cekin opened the "Cek-In Ark" motel and bar on the Sterling Highway at the junction with the road to Tustumena Lake. In 1989, Alton Priest bought the place and changed the name to "Big Al's Lodge." John and Suzie Cook bought the bar in 1991 and renamed it the Tustumena Lodge. The big steel "T" out in front of the bar provided an easy landmark and a nickname.

The Cook's began collecting and displaying hats and caps on the walls, rafters, and ceiling of the bar. The number of hats began at 135 when a friend died, and they inherited them. After 14 years of collecting, the count had reached 22,014. This was large enough for the Guinness Book of World Records to certify (on March 11, 2002) that the Tustumena Lodge had the largest collection of hats in the world. The hats and caps kept coming in from all over the world and the collection eventually numbered over 27,000. The Cook's sold the lodge to Duane Lafleur in 2005 and the record was broken the next year. The hats became somewhat of a burden, and a fire hazard, and were disposed of.

In 1994, the Tustumena Lodge became the new starting point for the Tustumena 200 sled dog race. The "T200" is a qualifying race for the Iditarod. The "T200" was due to celebrate 30 years in 2013 but was canceled that year and for the next three years due to lack of snow. The T200 now begins and ends in Ninilchik.

☞Visiting the Tustumena: Even though the hats are long gone, this Big T has persevered and is definitely worth a visit, particularly if you're hungry for a burger or want to play a game of pool. Drink specials are found here almost every day of the week.

Postcard from the Tustumena Lodge celebrating inclusion in the Guinness Book of World Records – 2003.

Que' Ana Bar
69940 (Mile 122.5) Sterling Highway, Kasilof (Clam Gulch)
(907) 567-3454

License Issued: October 20, 1976, to Robert and Dorothy Murray and Leonard and Hanna Stormo
Amenities: Pool table, TVs, food, occasional live music
Find them Online: Facebook

History and Notoriety: Corea Creek intersects the Sterling Highway here, and a bar known as the Corea Bend was at this location in 1959. Robert and Dorothy Murray bought the Corea Bend in 1972 and changed the name to the Corea Bar. They partnered with Leonard and Hanna Stormo in 1976 and changed the name to the Que' Ana Bar. Hanna Stormo is from the village of Akiak, and "que' ana" means "thank you" in her native Yupik language. The

Stormos became the sole owners in 1977. Leonard passed away in 2000 and Hanna sold the bar in 2002. April Halliday-Miller is the current owner.

In an interview in 2011, Hanna described life at the Que' Ana Bar. "We never had an official restaurant inside the bar, but people would bring covered dishes and we'd have potlucks all the time. In the summertime, all our relatives would come and camp out on the property for weeks at a time. It was so much fun."

The Que' Ana made quite an impression on Emily Johnson, the Stormos granddaughter. Johnson is now a professional dancer, and choreographed a performance called *The Thank-You Bar* which is about "a jukebox, a roadside bar, (and) a fish that never dies." She and her troupe have performed *The Thank-You Bar* in a variety of locations in the Lower 48, Montreal, Russia, and Alaska, including the Que' Ana Bar.

☛**Visiting the Que' Ana:** This bar calls itself the "Last of the Original Kenai Peninsula Roadhouses." One half of the bar resembles a living room and includes a wood stove, TV, easy chair, and a China hutch. There are lots of Alaskan crafts for sale here.

Alice's Champagne Palace
195 East Pioneer Avenue, Homer
(907) 226-2739

License Issued: January 23, 1980, to Alice Cochrane
Amenities: Pool table, TVs, food, occasional live music
Find them Online: https://www.aliceschampagnepalace.com/; Facebook

History and Notoriety: In 1958, the Club Bar was at this location, owned by Eugene Carlson. Goldie Steward bought the bar the following year and then sold it to Alice Cochrane in 1963. Alice, originally from California, moved to Alaska in 1951 and lived in Fairbanks, Seldovia, and finally Homer. She sold the Club Bar in 1975, right before a fire destroyed it. It was re-built, and the new owners celebrated by having a mural of a nude man and woman, with genitalia, painted on the front outer wall, causing a big controversy. (Towels were later painted over the genitals.)

Alice bought the bar back in 1980 and changed the name to Alice's Champagne Palace, a name she came up with while driving the Alaska Highway. Alice was described as a "free spirit" with a ready smile. She booked musicians like Elvin Bishop (famous for the song *Fooled Around and Fell in Love*) in 1988, and blues guitarist Jimmy Rogers (from the Muddy Waters Band) in 1990. She sold her champagne palace in 1998 to David and Trudy Ritchie and passed away in 2001.

The annual Homer "Poetry Slam" was held at Alice's from 1998 to 2002. Financial problems forced the closure of the bar in late 2004, and the bar was sold to the English Bay Corporation and reopened in 2005.

In 2009, a 70th birthday party was held at Alice's for Irwin Ravin, an Alaskan lawyer who intentionally got arrested in 1973 with marijuana in his pocket. He challenged and successfully changed the state's pot laws, which were decriminalized in 2014.

Ellis Paul, a folk musician, and classic urban songwriter, visited Homer and wrote a song about Alice's. A line in the chorus states "Raise a glass, tip the chalice, welcome to Alice's Champagne Palace. The finest bar in the strip in Homer, Alaska."

Alice's closed again in February 2014, which is why it wasn't included in the first edition of this book. It re-opened in December 2014 under new management with some major improvements: a new women's bathroom, a shiny copper front for the bar, a bigger back deck, and sixteen draft beer taps.

☛**Visiting Alice's Champagne Palace:** If you're in the mood for live music, Alice's is the most likely bar in Homer to have it, although you might have to pay a cover charge. Since it has re-opened, there are no more traditional bar games. Instead, there is an emphasis on food, with a full dinner menu available. I have never ordered champagne at Alice's, but the beer selection is awesome, including local beers brewed and sold only in Homer.

Alice Cochrane (1933 – 2001).
Photo by Lu Anna from Historical Homer *Facebook Group*

AJ's Oldtown Steakhouse and Tavern
(a.k.a. Waterfront)
120 West Bunnell Avenue, Homer
(907) 235-9949

License Issued: September 12, 1962, to Clinton E. and Margaret L. Sharp
Amenities: Food, occasional live music
Find them Online: https://www.ajsteakhouse.com/; Facebook

History and Notoriety: In 1941, this was the Homer Cafe and Club. In 1962, Harold and Electa Billups sold the bar to Clinton "Tex" and Margaret "Marg" Sharp who changed the name to Waterfront Bar and Dining. The bar is a block and a half from Bishops Beach, but the name endured. The Waterfront was owned by a succession of owners, including Rita Lochner who bought and sold the bar three times between 1976 and 1985. Jack Griffin, who also owned the Down East Saloon, bought the bar in 1986 and changed the name to Jack's Waterfront Dining Room and Lounge. It simply became the Waterfront Lounge in 1990.

William "Chip" Duggan became owner in 1999 and changed the name to Duggan's Waterfront. Duggan, from Minneapolis, and his wife Noreen, from Ireland, brought an Irish flavor to the bar, which helped improve its reputation. According to Duggan, the bar was referred to as the "Knife and Gun Club" because of the frequent conflicts between the clientele, such as the fishermen, construction workers, the Coast Guard "Coasties" and tourists.

Duggan sold the Waterfront to Alex and Adrienne Sweeney in 2011. Adrienne (nee Walli) was born and raised in Homer. Her great-grandmother Lillian Walli established the Homer Cash Store in 1936. The Sweeneys purchased the Driftwood Inn across the street in 2003 and decided to take a chance on the Waterfront.

> ☛**Visiting AJ's**: Some Homerites still refer to AJ's as the Waterfront, even though the atmosphere has changed dramatically. The restaurant is high-end for Homer and serves steaks and seafood. The bar is separate from the restaurant and is a good place to linger either before or after dinner.

From the Alaska Centennial – *1967.*

Down East Saloon
3125 East End Road, Homer
(907) 235-6002

License Issued: May 21, 1987, to Patrick Hickey
Amenities: Pool table, occasional live music
Find them Online: Facebook

History and Notoriety: Homerites refer to businesses in this area as being "down east" of Homer, although the bar is within the city limits. Pat Hickey sold the bar to George "Big George" Smith in 1991. Smith was originally from Indiana and came to Alaska in 1966. He owned several bars in Anchorage and in Homer, including the Waterfront, Bayside, Yah Sure Club, and Jack's Other Place. Smith passed away in 2003, and his ashes are still stored at the Down East. Jack "Big Jack" Griffin and Earl Kramer bought the bar in 1993. Griffin died in 2003, and Kramer in 2016. Justin Cole is the current owner.

Earl Kramer told me that in the 1990s, actor Ernest Borgnine and media mogul Ted Turner both visited the Down East. The bar has a tradition of employing primarily women bartenders.

☛**Visiting the Down East Saloon:** The backyard has a stage, which is a sweet spot to listen to music in the summer months. The Independence Day Pig Roast, Super Bowl, Cinco de Mayo, Octoberfest, and Halloween are popular times to be at the Down East.

Salty Dawg Saloon
(a.k.a. The Dawg)
4380 Homer Spit Road, Homer
(907) 235-6718

License Issued: 1957 to Charles Abbott and James Neely
Amenities: Pool table, occasional live music
Find them Online: https://saltydawgsaloon.com/; Facebook

History and Notoriety: The Salty Dawg is one of just three bars in Alaska that have had an entire book written specifically about it (the Alaskan in Juneau and the Yukon Inn in Galena are the other two). I have borrowed liberally from the pages of *The Dawg's Tale* by Diane Ford Wood for what follows.

The end of the Homer Spit was where the original coal town of Homer was located back in 1896, but it had been abandoned in 1902 due to the decline in the coal market. The "new" town of Homer was relocated to the base of the spit in 1916. When Charles "Chuck" and Phyllis Abbott and Jim Neely decided to open a bar way out at the end of the spit, 5 miles from town, folks thought it laughable. The Abbotts decorated the bar in a pirate theme to honor "the original salty dawgs" while Jim Neely served as bartender. They sold the bar in 1962 to Earl and Mary Jane Hillstrand, who owned the nearby Land's End Resort.

There are three small log buildings that comprise the Salty Dawg. The main bar building was built around 1897, and once housed a grocery store, post office, and the offices of the Cook Inlet Coal Fields Company. The adjoining room dates to 1909 and was originally a barn and later a schoolhouse. Prior to 1927, the current storeroom was in town and used as a post office, and for a short time the Salty Pup café. The "lighthouse" tower was added after the 1964 earthquake and houses the pool table. In 1975, the tower became an official navigational landmark and is shown on nautical charts.

In the early days of the Dawg, there was an outhouse behind the bar. On one occasion, the men's side became backed up, and Chuck Abbott hired a local miner to help. The miner decided that two sticks of dynamite were in order. The explosion blew the toilet contents all over the end of the spit!

The 1964 earthquake caused the spit to sink, which meant that when the tide came in, customers at the Dawg would watch the water cover the floor. Earl Hillstrand moved the Dawg to its current location.

Earl Hillstrand died in 1974, and the Dawg was bought by Loree McGee and Robert Sykes. John Warren took over in 1980, and he and his wife Lynn and son John L. still own and manage the Dawg.

☛**Visiting the Salty Dawg**: This is one of the most famous bars in Alaska and is a must-see when in Homer. Bring a dollar bill, business card, or undergarment to add to the collection. Note the human skull on the wall behind the bar. During the summer months, tourists and locals rub elbows at this bar. I was approached at the Dawg (with my parents in tow) by a man who insisted that he and I used to work on a fishing boat out of English Bay. Sometimes, it's better just to agree and go along with the story. Memorial Day weekend, Independence Day, Halloween, and New Year's Eve are popular times to be at the Dawg.

A Guide to the Notorious Bars of Alaska

From *Alaska Highway Sketches* by Connie Silver – 1961.

Linwood Bar
(a.k.a. The Wood)
253 Main Street, Seldovia
(907) 630-0573

License Issued: 1946 to Carl Nordenson
Amenities: Pool table, food, occasional live music, liquor store
Find them Online: https://www.linwoodbar.com/; Facebook

History and Notoriety: In 1940, Carl Nordenson, from Sweden, was working in a salmon cannery in Seldovia. By 1946, he had opened the Linwood Bar which included the Linwood Café, which was managed separately. By 1948, the bar included a dance hall. Clinton "Shorty" and Pearl Bailey bought the Linwood in October of 1952 and the Bailey family would own the bar for the next twenty years.

Elsa Pederson, an author who lived in Seldovia during the post WWII years, recalled the excitement caused by "fishermen with too much money and so few women in town." She explained that "trouble usually started in the Linwood or the Surf Club. If the dispute was between a Seldovian and an 'outsider' the fight usually drew in combatants from both sides, with fist fights up and down the boardwalk."

The 1964 earthquake caused the Seldovia area to sink. When the high tide came in, the floor of the Linwood would flood, and people would have to sit on top of the tables. "Shorty" Bailey solved this problem by rowing a boat from the bar to each table to serve the drinks! The bar was eventually rebuilt at its current location.

During the 1970s and '80s, the Linwood competed with the Seldovia Lodge and the Knight Spot (the three bars were known locally as the "Iron Triangle.") Fist fights between the fishermen and loggers were common in all three bars. According to one account, the opposing forces decided to exchange jobs for a day, which forever ended the feud.

In 1972, Iona Hutcheson (daughter of the Baileys) and John "Greasy" Colberg Jr. bought the bar. John and his wife Alta "Patty" Colberg took over in 1973 but sold to Robert and Mary Van Winkle in 1982. By 1993, the Colbergs were the owners again. Stephanie Blanchard, from Chile, bought the bar in 2013 and is the current owner.

In 1958, a bottle of Olympia beer was auctioned off at the Firemen's Ball which was held at the Linwood. Thus began the tradition of auctioning off the unopened bottle. Bids have ranged from twenty-five dollars to over four thousand dollars. In past years, winning bidders would take the liquid trophy all over town. The still unopened bottle is banned from parading. Funds raised have been used for a defibrillator, a hip replacement for a longtime Seldovia resident, and a new fire truck and ambulance.

☛**Visiting the Linwood Bar:** The Linwood is not the rough and tumble bar it was but is still a great place to have a drink and a bite to eat. Seldovia does a righteous Independence Day celebration, and the deck at the Linwood is the place to be.

Tips Bar
12349 Old Glenn Highway, Eagle River
(907) 694-2372

License Issued: 1953 to G.C. Manning and Oswald J. McGann
Amenities: Pool tables, darts, TVs, food, occasional live music
Find them Online: Facebook

History and Notoriety: The first automobile bridge over Eagle River was constructed in 1933, but the Glenn Highway connecting Anchorage with Palmer wasn't completed until 1942. G.C. "Pete" Manning and Oswald "Mac" McGann, decided to build Tips to serve the travelers and the homesteaders in the Eagle River valley. The bar was a sponsor of the first Chugiak Spring Carnival in 1954. By 1970, the Glenn Highway had been re-routed around downtown Eagle River, but Tips has endured and is one of the oldest businesses in town.

Herbert Were bought Tips in 1966 and then sold it to Palmer Hogelie and James Welch in 1971. Palmer' wife Patricia worked as a bartender and the couple ran the bar for over twenty years, taking on partners Billy "Pete" and Carole Estep in 1978. The Esteps took full control in 1992 and owned Tips for 26 years. Pete died in 2017 and Carole in 2018. Howard and Chun Mo Shim are the current owners.

From 1984 – 1986, there was a second Tips Bar, known as Tips Too, located in nearby Chugiak.

☛**Visiting Tips Bar:** This bar is popular with bikers. Many bachelor and bachelorette parties and wedding receptions have been held here, as well as an incredible number of wakes and celebrations of life.

Birchwood Saloon
20146 Pilots Road, Chugiak
(907) 688-2827

License issued: June 11, 1995, to Daniel and Wanda Gates
Amenities: Pool tables, darts, ping pong, food, occasional live music, liquor store
Find them Online: Facebook

History and Notoriety: In 1976, there were only two bars in Chugiak when Galen and Frances Atwater opened the Mt. McKinley Pilots Grille, which is now the Birchwood Saloon. Galen was born in Maine in 1928, served in the Army and Navy, and moved to Alaska in 1954. Frances "Fran" was born in 1924 in Florida, and hitchhiked solo (!) to Alaska in 1950.

In 1980, the Atwater's twenty-six-year-old son Jack was tragically electrocuted by a high-voltage power line while working on the roof of the Co-Pilot Motel adjacent to the Pilots Grille. Two years later, the Atwater' sold the bar to Eddie James (see Eddie's Sports

Bar) but bought it back in 1987, renaming it the Mt. McKinley View Lounge. They sold it to Daniel and Wanda Gates in 1995, who changed the name to the Birchwood Saloon. Chugiak is in Birchwood, a community within the Municipality of Anchorage.

The Birchwood Saloon is believed by many to be haunted, specifically by the ghost of Jack Atwater. Wanda Gates was the bookkeeper for the Pilot's Bar and remembers Jack as "always dressed in blue jeans and a blue flannel shirt." She says that the ghost of Jack is not threatening and will make his presence known by turning on the stereo, turning lights on and off, opening doors, and moving pool balls around. At least four parties of paranormal investigators have spent the night at the saloon and have recorded ghostly images and even voices.

In 1999, the rock band ZZ Top performed in Anchorage and then visited the Birchwood Saloon. It's unknown whether the band utilized the Z-shaped pool table, which was purchased from the Alyeska ski resort.

☛**Visiting the Birchwood Saloon:** The saloon is popular with bikers and owners of classic cars. It is roomy, has a dance floor, and a large "VIP table" with a marble top. The outdoor beer garden is a nice spot to be on a sunny day.

Palmer Bar
828 South Colony Way, Palmer
(907) 745-3041

License Issued: 1936 to Bernard and Alice Reitan
Amenities: Pool table, darts, TVs, food, occasional live music
Find them Online: Facebook

History and Notoriety: Bernard and Alice Reitan, from Wisconsin, and their two children were among the very first farmer colonists at Matanuska Valley in May of 1935. The following year, the couple opened a beer dispensary on the opposite side (wrong side) of the railroad tracks from the Palmer colony.

"We sell the milk, they sell the booze" the colonists would remark, although they themselves were also known to imbibe. The bar was first located in the basement of Bert's Drug Store, but by 1941, the Palmer Cocktail Bar had its own spot next door to Bert's Liquor Store. Neal and Marie Wright, who owned Bert's, were the owners from 1945 – 1951. The bar burned to the ground in 1948. The Wright's sold it to Bob and Ruth Peterson, who moved the bar to its current location in 1960. The bar had a succession of owners until 1983 when Mary Lou Coddington and her son Jack Burnett bought it. They owned the bar for 37 years, long enough for people to call it Lou-Jack's. Coddington and Burnett sold the bar to Wesley Artz and Sherman Liefer in 2020.

In 1974, Hiram Walker Inc., the makers of Canadian Club Whiskey, awarded the Palmer Bar its "My Favorite Tavern" award. Enough customers petitioned the company which led to an official visit by a representative and the presentation of an "elegant scroll."

☛**Visiting the Palmer Bar**: This historic bar is a good place to be when you're hungry, as they serve burgers almost all day long. The Palmer Colony Days celebration in June is a busy time at the bar.

The Palmer Bar before the 1948 fire.
Wallace J. Wellenstein Collection; Anchorage Museum, B2017.023.083

Klondike Mike's Saloon
820 South Colony Way, Palmer
(907) 745-2676

License Issued: June 6, 1983, to Douglas Nielson, Mark Hartman, and Michael Folkerth
Amenities: Pool tables, darts, TVs, food, occasional live music
Find them Online: Facebook

History and Notoriety: Klondike Mike's has its roots in a bar located here in 1956 known as the 49er Club and in 1978 as Lee Roy's 49er Club. The 49er was notorious and was a known hangout for rowdies. The saloon was named after partner "Klondike Mike" Folkerth, an experienced bush pilot who barely escaped death after his float plane flipped upside-down after landing in a lake the year before buying the bar. "The experience," Folkert said, "has taught me to not dwell on the little things in life, but to focus on the much bigger picture—don't get caught majoring in the minors."

People in Anchorage (and even certain politicians) have been known to refer to the folks living in Palmer and Wasilla as "valley trash." Klondike Mike's embraced this moniker with their Proud-To-Be-Valley-Trash party, which gave prizes to costumes made of tarps, duct tape, bubble wrap etc. This bar has also hosted the occasional wet T-shirt contest, Jello-wrestling event, "Prom Night" and "Pimp and Ho" parties.

The restaurant adjoining the bar is now Garcia's Grill, which serves Mexican Food.

☛**Visiting Klondike Mike's:** This bar is popular with the college-age crowd. Note the large amount of graffiti on the walls. The bathrooms, however, are immaculate.

Moosehead Saloon
808 South Colony Way, Palmer
(907) 746-2299

License issued: June 21, 1986, to Harold and Marilyn Sellick
Amenities: Pool tables, dart board, TVs, food, occasional live music
Find them Online: Facebook

History and Notoriety: In 1984, Bob Chace owned the Chace Lounge in Palmer, located at 708 South Alaska Way. In 1985, he renovated the building by giving it a false front, which made it look like an old west saloon. The following year, he sold the lounge to Harold "Hal" Sellick and his wife Marilyn, who changed the name to the Moosehead Saloon. The Sellick' decorated the interior of the saloon with antiques, a real moose head, and a custom bar with picture top. Hal was born in Canada in 1937, had lived in Arizona, and moved to Alaska in 1980. Marilyn had also lived in Arizona and was a Palmer Councilwoman in 1996.

Fans of Hobo Jim (real name Jim Varsos) remember the Moosehead Saloon as the place where in 1989 the musician played non-stop for 18 hours and 10 minutes. Someone asked Hobo how long he could go without a break, which led to his marathon at the Moosehead. He started at 8 am and didn't stop until after 2 am, playing over 450 songs, never repeating a single one. "Looking back on it, the only thing I remember was that it was a really stupid thing to do," he said later. Hobo Jim lost his life to cancer in 2021.

In October 1990, Hal and Marilyn moved the Moosehead to the next block south at 808 South Colony Way. Tragically, Hal died from an accidental fire at home in 1996. Marilyn sold the bar to Daniel and Kyna DeBoer in 2002.

☛**Visiting the Moosehead Saloon**: While the historic feel of the old saloon is gone, the Moosehead is still a fun place to be, particularly on St. Patrick's Day, Halloween, and New Years Eve. Its proximity to the Klondike Saloon and the Palmer Bar makes it a great place to begin, or end, a Palmer bar crawl.

Fishhook Bar
(a.k.a. The Hook)
9231 North Palmer-Fishhook Road, Palmer
(907) 745-6374

License Issued: January 31, 1979, to James R. Byers
Amenities: Pool table, darts, TVs, food, occasional live music
Find them Online: https://fishhookbarandgrill.com/; Facebook

History and Notoriety: This area of Palmer has been known as Fishhook since 1910. The Carle Wagon Road (now Wasilla-Fishhook Road) was built in 1907 to carry freight from Knik to the Independence Mine and is the oldest road in the valley. The Fishhook Bar is located at "the Y" where the two Fishhook Roads, Wasilla, and North Palmer, meet and become the road to Hatcher Pass.

Jim Byers owned the bar for only a year before selling it to his sister Ruth Page and her husband Darrell. Darrell passed away in 1999 and Ruth owned the bar until 2021. Kimberly Levesque is the current owner.

The bar is one of the oldest businesses in Fishhook and is truly an institution. It is a favorite of fishermen and for skiers going to or coming from Hatcher Pass.

> **Visiting the Fishhook Bar:** This is a good place to come and hear local bands on the weekends. The bar is known for its burgers, but breakfast is also served.

Alpine Inn
Mile 61 Glenn Highway, Palmer (Sutton)
(907) 745-9955

License issued: 1945 to Henry, Michael, and Francis O'Neill
Amenities: Pool tables, dart board, TVs, food, occasional live music
Find them Online: Facebook

History and Notoriety: Henry "Harry" O'Neill was born in North Dakota in 1885 and was living in Cordova in 1908. By 1945, Harry and his sons Michael "Mike" and Francis "Jack" owned the Richmond and the Victory cocktail bars in Anchorage and decided that the Sutton area would be a good place for another one. The

Glenn Highway had officially opened for travelers in 1943 and production at the nearby Jonesville Coal Mine was peaking. The Alpine Inn included cabins for lodging, and a restaurant.

The bar had been open for just a year when three armed bandits dressed in military clothing robbed the bar of eight hundred dollars. This happened in front of fifteen customers, most of whom were miners.

Ads from the early 1950s tout the Alpine Inn as being the place "for dining, for dancing, for refreshments." Mike O'Neill had become the primary owner, but by 1957 brother Phillip "Phil" and his wife Jean had taken over. The coal miners, most of them bachelors, would come into Sutton for the weekend. Phil recalled: "We'd start working Friday night, I at the bar and my wife in the kitchen, and we wouldn't even stop 'til Monday." The Jonesville mine closed in 1967.

On January 20, 1968, a very pregnant woman on her way to the hospital in Palmer stopped at the Alpine Inn, lay down on one of the pool tables and gave birth to a boy. She named him Alpine Kameroff, and the boy grew up to become the assistant fire chief for the community of Kenny Lake. The loved and respected Alpine Kameroff died tragically in a car accident on the Glenn Highway in 2004.

In 1971, a fire destroyed the main building, and the owners sold the bar back to the O'Neill family. It burned down again in December 1981 and re-opened ten months later. James Psenak bought the bar in 2010 and is the current owner.

In 1986, the Alpine Inn held the first Coal Miners Ball which included entertainment, live music, and food. The annual event is held on the last Saturday of June.

In 2008, Alaskan actor, director, and writer Levi Taylor used the Alpine Inn for the bar scene in a short film titled *Way up North*. The film has been described as Robert Service meets Quentin Tarantino. The film won an award for "Best Editing" at the 2009 Beverly Hills Film Festival.

☛**Visiting the Alpine Inn:** The name of this Census designated place is Sutton-Alpine. This classic Alaskan bar is the unofficial community center of Sutton. It is a large bar, and the backyard and deck are the place to be on a sunny day. Take in the Coal Miners Ball and plan to spend the night locally.

From *Lou Jacobin's* Guide to Alaska and the Yukon – *1961*.

Alaskan Hotel Bar (Cordova)
600 First Street (First and B Avenue), Cordova
(907) 424-3299

License issued: June 1933, to Fannie Ferrell
Amenities: Pool table, shuffleboard, darts, occasional live entertainment, food, liquor store
Find them Online: Facebook

History and Notoriety: The MacCormac Hotel was built in the summer of 1908 while Cordova was preparing to become the terminus of the Copper River and Northwestern Railroad. In late September, a café and hotel bar opened on the first floor. In August of 1915, the name changed to the Alaskan Hotel. Robert Ferrell, from Texas, bought the hotel in 1921. His wife Frances "Fannie" who was born in Riga, Latvia, oversaw the café and, after prohibition, the bar. The *Cordova Daily Times* reported on May 15, 1933, that beer would soon be for sale in town and that "A special place is being fitted up at the Alaska(n) Hotel where the 'flowing beverage' will be dispensed."

The town that was not chosen to be the terminus of the railroad was Katalla, located fifty air miles southeast of Cordova. The Alaskan obtained a beautiful mahogany "Waldorf" style back bar from the liquidating Hotel Northern in Katalla. In 1941, the back bar was pried loose from the wall. Over a gallon of pennies spilled out, having been tossed there by bartenders to take them out of circulation because they were too small of a denomination. The back bar is today the best-preserved piece of the ghost town of Katalla.

Fannie passed away in 1945, and ownership of the hotel and bar passed to her nephews Robert "Bob" and Bernard Leff. Bob was working at the hotel as a clerk in 1940, and by 1947 he was the sole owner. In 1960, he sold the Alaskan to James "Jim" and Vivian

Nichols and Robert "Kernel" Korn. Vivian was once quoted as saying, 'The years in the bar business were a lesson in human nature and behavior that would fill volumes."

Jim Nichols and partners Bill (son of Vivian from a previous marriage) and Linda McCullough took over in 1963. Also, that year, the hotel survived a fire that destroyed many buildings on Main Street. It also survived the 1964 earthquake. The bar was sold in 1981 to Lew and Lelia Cochran, who sold it to David Chipman and Cheryl Lewis in 1989. Chipman and Lewis are still the owners.

The Alaskan is noted for its lighted sign, with all three panels mounted upside down. The story goes that it was accidentally installed this way. It was decided to leave it as it is, so that a drunk person waking face-up on the sidewalk would be able to realize where they are.

☛**Visiting the Alaskan:** When having a drink at the Alaskan, it becomes clear why several artists have sketched it. The entire bar is made of wood, including the floor, which gives it a distinctive, historic look. The Alaskan is a busy place during the Cordova Iceworm Festival in February.

Fannie Ferrell (1870 – 1945).

*Bernard (left) and Bob Leff.
Photos courtesy of Cheryl Lewis*

Powder House Bar and Grill
1418 (Mile 1.5) Copper River Highway, Cordova
(907) 424-3529

License issued: 1953 to Robert W. Korn and Pierre J. de Ville
Amenities: Darts, ping pong, TVs, food, occasional live entertainment
Find them Online: Facebook

History and Notoriety: Robert "Kernel" Korn, born in Missouri in 1891, was a postal clerk in Cordova in 1930. He would later own the Imperial bar and co-own the Alaskan Hotel bar. The

Bob Korn Memorial Swimming Pool in Cordova and a nearby mountain are named in his honor. Pierre de Ville, born in Katalla in 1908, was a son of Pierre E. "French Pete" de Ville, discoverer of the Paris lode claim which became the famous Treadwell Mine on Douglas Island near Juneau. "French Pete" invested his entire estate in the town of Katalla, believing it would become the railroad terminus for the Copper River and Northwestern Railroad. He lost it all when Cordova was chosen and died in 1911.

Korn and de Ville opened the Powder House on land adjacent to where the "powder house" for the railroad was once located. Blasting powder was used in abundance during the building of the railroad, and the slogan "I got blasted at the Powder House" became popular in the 1980s—the fishing boom years of Cordova. Korn passed away in 1972, and de Ville and his wife Zelma became the owners and lived upstairs over the bar. They sold the bar to Enok and Libbie Lian in 1984, and Libbie became the owner in 1993. Libbie would encourage fishermen to bring their catch to the bar. She would cook the fish and provide the side dishes. She sold the bar to Robin Traxinger in 2022.

☞**Visiting the Powder House:** The bar is a big supporter of the Cordova Iceworm Festival in February; the "Shuck and Suck" oyster shucking contest on Saturday night of the festival is a must see. The deck, which overlooks Eyak Lake, is an awesome place to be on a sunny day.

Bob "Kernel" Korn (1891 – 1972).
Photo courtesy of Cheryl Lewis

Mug-Shot Saloon
251 West Parks Highway, Wasilla
(907) 376-1617

License issued: June 22, 1989, to Marilyn and Theodore Anderson Jr.
Amenities: Pool tables, darts, TVs, horseshoes, cornhole, volleyball, food, occasional live music
Find them Online: Facebook

History and Notoriety: This bar began as the Holiday Lodge in 1976. By 1981, it was Huppie's Road House. Huppie's (named for owner Robert Hupert, pronounced who-pees) was a wild and crazy place in the 1980s. It was where folks went when the Anchorage bars closed at 2:30 a.m. (Wasilla bars stay open until 5 a.m.). The Mug-Shot has carried on the tradition of Huppie's and provides a central place to party for Valley dwellers.

Above the horseshoe shaped bar are caricature drawings of patrons, past and present. Many of these drawings date back to the Huppie days. The more recent drawings have been made to look like mug shots.

The most famous resident of Wasilla is Sarah Palin, who served as its mayor from 1996 – 2002 (as conservative as Palin appears to be, she did not change the bar closing hours). The Mug-Shot was a big supporter of Palin and provided live coverage of her speech at the 2008 Republican National Convention and her debate with fellow vice-presidential candidate Joe Biden. Mug-Shot owner Marilyn Anderson observed that the bar patrons were spellbound and joked to a *Washington Post* reporter that "They weren't drinking enough, dammit." During that time, the Andersons were inundated with phone calls from reporters, all looking for dirt on Palin.

Since 2010, the Mug-Shot has thrown an annual party in August known as the "Big M" which is held in memory of Marilyn Anderson, who died in 2009 fighting a rare form of cancer. The fundraising event invites merchants to the party, with all proceeds going to a local resident who is currently undergoing cancer treatment. This very popular outdoor event features an auction, lots of food, and live music. Theodore "Ted" Anderson died in 2023, and per his request, the Mug-Shot celebrated his passing with a "Dead Ted's Last Fiasco" party.

☛Visiting the Mug-Shot Saloon: Sports fans love the bar because of the many TVs. I have always liked the big backyard with the horseshoe pits and the volleyball court. The bar celebrates all the usual holidays and is very fond of theme parties (be sure to check out their Facebook page).

Knik Bar
(a.k.a. Broken Boat Bar)
10204 (Mile 13.5) South Knik-Goose Bay Road, Wasilla
(907) 376-3818

License issued: 1957 to Melvin K. and Lois L. Bjorn
Amenities: Pool table, TVs, food, occasional live music, liquor store
Find them Online: Facebook

History and Notoriety: Known first as the Knik Lake Bar, it served the early homesteaders, including Joe Redington, Sr., who founded the Iditarod Trail Sled Dog Race. Melvin died in 1964, and Lois Bjorn took on partners Frank and Arlene Brown, who took full control of the bar in 1968. Clyda Hallstead, James Welch, and Palmer Hogelie bought the bar in 1977. The trio changed the name to simply the Knik Bar. By this time, Knik Lake was known as the official restart location of the Iditarod Trail Sled Dog Race.

Iditarod, the most famous sled dog race in the world, began in 1973. From 1973 – 2007, after the ceremonial start in Anchorage, Knik Lake was the race restart location. This brought an incredible number of people to Knik Lake, and the Knik Bar. Edward and Darlene Donnelly, who became the owners in 1996, had to hire thirty extra people every year to handle "Iditarod Sunday," which included tending the bar, waiting tables and manning two minibars.

Beth Bragg, a reporter for the *Anchorage Daily News*, was at the Knik Bar for the restart in 2002. She described the throngs of people coming to witness the restart, including the hundreds of cars parked on frozen Knik Lake. That day, the bar featured entertainment by Hobo Jim (real name Jim Varsos, 1952 – 2021) which was his eighteenth restart performance. "It's the Mardi Gras of winter" he said. "This is one of my favorites of the year." Unfortunately, 2002 was the last year the restart was held at Knik Lake. Primarily because of the lack of snow, it was moved permanently to Willow in 2008. Knik Lake is now home to the Knik 100 and Knik 200 Sled Dog Races.

A reminder of Joe Redington, Sr., is visible from the Knik Bar. The *Nomad*, a wooden boat used by Redington for hauling fish until 1968, was parked in a hayfield that was thought to be above the high tide line. True to its name, the *Nomad* used to move with the tides, but it has found a permanent resting place. See The Nomad Restoration group on Facebook.

☛**Visiting the Knik Bar:** The bar serves pizza and burgers most days and steaks on Friday night. An outdoor beer garden beckons in the summer months. The bar celebrates the birthday of Hobo Jim on December 21st.

Tug Bar
(a.k.a. Goose Bay Inn)
Mile 18.5 Knik-Goose Bay Road, Wasilla
(907) 376-5720

License issued: September 28, 1993, to Patsy K. Monsen
Amenities: Pool table, darts, TVs, food, occasional live music, liquor store
Find them Online: Facebook (Tug Bar Goose Bay Inn)

History and Notoriety: Back in 1969, the bar that was at this out-of-the-way location was Dooley's Diner and Bar. Other the next 24 years the name would change to Mac's Place, the Truckin' Duck, Blackie's Place, and the Goose Bay Bar. In 1993, Patsy Monsen changed its name to the Tug Bar and then sold it in 1997 to

Tim Cornelius. Cornelius is a former Captain from the Anchorage Fire Department who bought the Tug after losing his house in the Miller's Reach Fire of 1996.

Some people associate the Tug Bar with the Klondike 300 sled dog race. The Klondike was a three-hundred-mile race that was held annually and began and ended at the Tug. The race hasn't been held since 2009 due to the lack of snow. Since 2018, the Goose Bay 150 sled dog race begins and ends at the Tug.

The slogan for the Tug Bar used to be "Where the pavement ends, the fun begins." But since the entire road is now paved, it's more like "Where the pavement used to end, the fun still happens," according to Terri Cornelius, wife of Tim.

The Tug is popular with bikers and several benefit rides have ended at the bar.

☞Visiting the Tug Bar: The Tug has a beautiful fenced-in grassy yard complete with tables and umbrellas, a fire pit, and a covered stage where live music can be found every weekend during the summer. Check out Taco Tuesdays and the Sunday Barbecue.

Silver Fox Inn
8431 (Mile 50) West Parks Highway, Wasilla
(907) 892-6179

License Issued: April 13, 1984, to Henry F. and Wanda Dunaway

Amenities: Pool tables, dart boards, food, occasional live music, motel

Find them Online: Facebook

History and Notoriety: Henry "Hank" Dunaway was born in Missouri in 1923. After serving in the Army during WWII, he married Wanda in 1948 and moved to California. The couple moved to Anchorage in 1950, and then to Wasilla in 1979, while Hank worked as a contractor on construction projects.

In 1984, Hank and Wanda opened the Silver Fox Inn. Friends of Hank started calling him "Silver Fox" due to his hair turning prematurely gray, and the name seemed appropriate for the bar as well. Hank's love of pool and darts was evident from the beginning, with several tables and boards positioned strategically around the bar. Hank passed away in 1992, and Wanda sold the bar to Cassandra J. Alley in 1995.

In 2007, thieves broke into the bar and took an ATM machine. According to Alley, the machine was empty of cash and displaying an "Out of service" message on its screen. "Out of service, that means there's no money in it. They can't even read" she said of the culprits. Apparently, the thieves never saw the first *Barbershop* movie (2002) where a thief, played by Anthony Anderson, steals an ATM (also empty) and tries unsuccessfully to open it.

In 2008, a team of pool players from the Silver Fox, who called themselves the *Psycho Destroyers,* placed fifth out of 500 teams at the International 8-Ball Championships in Las Vegas, NV. The *Psycho Destroyers* won $3,900, split among the five players and two substitutes. Another men's team from the Silver Fox, the *Crazy 8s,* also competed.

☛Visiting the Silver Fox Inn: The bar is still very popular with the pool and darts crowd and will occasionally host tournaments, which will cancel live music. Be sure to check their Facebook page. Steak night on Fridays is a good reason to visit this bar.

Pioneer Lodge
33900 (Mile 71.4) Parks Highway, Willow
(907) 495-6884

License Issued: 1970 to Arthur W. Smith
Amenities: Food, occasional live music
Find them Online: Facebook; also Burnt Toast

History and Notoriety: Art "Smitty" Smith was born in New York state in 1927 and was living in Anchorage in 1950. He moved to Willow in 1968 and in 1970 opened the Pioneer Lodge at the south end of the Willow airstrip. The Parks Highway was still being constructed, and the airstrip was being used frequently. The lodge was open less than a year when it burned down in January 1971.

Smith then bought land where the new highway would cross Willow Creek and rebuilt the lodge, this time with a massive stone fireplace. The new Pioneer Lodge was open in May of 1972, with ads stating that it was the "new lodge with the old spirits." In 1978, the Pioneer hosted politician Wray E. "Brad" Bradley with a spaghetti luncheon. Bradley, who was running for Lieutenant Governor of Alaska, presented Willow citizens with a sign that read "Welcome to Willow: Capital of Alaska." Alaskans voted in 1976 to move the state capital from Juneau to Willow. However, funding for the move was voted down in 1982.

In 1980, two men were wounded in what was described as "a spectacular gunfight" inside the Pioneer Lodge. Both men emptied their revolvers at each other and when it was over, one man had wounds in his arm, neck and chest. The other man had part of his nose blown off by a .44 magnum slug. Both men were arrested and charged with reckless endangerment of human life. When asked about the cause of the argument, State Troopers said it was "the usual thing, nothing very important."

In 1992, Steve and Gwen White bought the lodge and added an RV Park to the business. Curtis and Linda Stillwell took over management in 1995 and bought the lodge in 2005. The main lodge building burned down the day after Labor Day in 2009. Linda Stillwell told me that the bar reopened using "two 55-gallon drums, a door for a table, a cooler, and a microphone for karaoke." The bar eventually moved into the building that was previously the bait shop, where it remains today. The old stone fireplace—dubbed "The Phoenix"—is occasionally used for outdoor parties.

☛**Visiting the Pioneer Lodge:** The popularity of the Pioneer increased in 2024 when the Burnt Toast kitchen opened adjacent to the lodge. People can take their food into the lodge and enjoy drinks, karaoke, and live music on weekends.

Fairview Inn
101 North Main Street, Talkeetna
(907) 733-2423

License issued: 1934 to Bruno Nauman
Amenities: Shuffleboard, foosball, TV, occasional live music
Find them Online: https://fairviewtalkeetna.com/; Facebook

History and Notoriety: The Alaska Railroad built a station at Talkeetna in 1920. The Fairview Inn offered rooms and hot meals by 1923, which was the sixth year of Alaska's prohibition. The area of the inn that is now the bar was used as the lobby and a small store. That same year, President Warren G. Harding travelled to Alaska, and took the Alaska Railroad from Seward to Fairbanks. On July 15, 1923, he drove a gold spike at Nenana that symbolized the completion of the railroad. After visiting Fairbanks, Harding, the First Lady and his entourage (including Secretary of Commerce and future President Herbert Hoover) took the train back to Seward on July 17. On that day, the party stopped in Talkeetna and visited the Fairview Inn. Bruno "Ben" Nauman, born in Germany and owner of the Fairview, asked the President to sign a dollar bill that he later framed and hung in the store. Harding died 16 days later in San Francisco, probably from a heart attack. It is unlikely that the President had an alcoholic beverage at the Fairview, and that his visit to Talkeetna had anything to do with his death but stories to the contrary persist to this day.

By 1934, Nauman had a dispensary license, allowing him to serve beer and wine. He sold liquor out of a separate building. He sold the Fairview to Carl Durand and John Campbell in 1939, who in turn sold it to Horace and Jessamine Nagley in 1940, owners of the local store. The Fairview changed hands a couple more times before being bought by Joseph Cook and Frank Moennikes in 1951, who turned the lobby into a bar.

Moennikes, born in Germany, moved to Talkeetna in 1934 and had been a miner. He would own the Fairview with four different sets of partners before finally selling it in 1973. In 1975, Moennikes was approached by a newspaper reporter from Anchorage who exclaimed that he must have seen a lot of changes in Talkeetna over his forty-one years. Moennikes responded with a simple "No." Moennikes passed away in 1984, and the resident ghost at the Fairview is presumed to be him.

Another colorful Talkeetna old timer was Jim Beaver. Kenny Holland, a local pilot, told the story that Beaver knew that the basement in the Fairview flooded every spring. There was a trapdoor behind the bar that opened into the basement, and on one occasion, Beaver decided to throw a bunch of live fish into the flooded basement. He knew there were tourists at the Fairview, so later that day he came into the bar with his fishing pole, took a seat next to the trapdoor, opened it, and said "Guess I'll do a little fishing." He proceeded to drink at the bar and catch fish, much to the amazement of the tourists.

The spur road to Talkeetna from the Parks Highway opened in 1965. Since then, the town has become popular with tourists and with those who want to climb Denali. The Fairview is the traditional place for climbers to gather before and after their climb. Behind the bar is a large mural of the mountain. Every climbing season, tiny international flags get pinned to it, symbolizing the nationalities represented on the mountain. There is also a corner of the bar that is dedicated to those that have perished climbing Denali. The Fairview was listed on the National Register of Historic Places on May 7, 1982. Henrik Wessel and Hans Axelsson bought the Fairview in 2022.

Visiting the Fairview Inn: No visit to Talkeetna is complete without a stop at the Fairview. Note the many photos on the walls and the antiques (piano, cash register, slot machine, canned goods). Visiting celebrities included musician John Denver and comedian Pauly Shore. The Moose Dropping Festival in July and the Winterfest in December are popular times to be at the Fairview.

From Talkeetna Cronies *by Nola H. Campbell.*

Talkeetna Inn
(a.k.a. Tee Pee Oasis Lounge; a.k.a. The Tavern)
22328 South B Street, Talkeetna
(907) 733-2323

License issued: 1964 to Alice S. Powell
Amenities: Pool table, TV, food
Find them Online: https://talkeetnainn.com/

History and Notoriety: Sherman Powell, born in Ohio in 1899, and his wife Alice, born in New York in 1907, were living in Anchorage in 1950. While "Sherm" was working for the Alaska

Railroad, Alice was working as a sanitation officer, which included inspecting restaurants and houses of prostitution. Her efficiency at this job earned her the nickname "Evil Alice" from the café owners and working girls. By 1960, the couple decided to move to Talkeetna and open the Talkeetna Motel. This was before the spur road to Talkeetna from the Parks Highway was completed in 1965. When the pavement ended just shy of the motel, Evil Alice paid to have it extended. The motel had two A-frame buildings: one was the dining hall where she served gourmet meals, and the other was the bar which she named the "Charlet Room." The name never caught on because locals thought the building looked like a "teepee."

Sherman Powell passed away in 1972, but Alice continued to manage the motel, restaurant and bar. She sold the complex to Ray and June Gerrish in 1976, who added partners LeRoy and Blanche Ickes. In 1980, Alfred and Patricia Sousa became the new owners.

"Al" was born in California in 1930, and "Pat" was born in Florida in 1929. They ran ads for the Talkeetna Motel in the *Anchorage Daily News* that described the "unique restaurant & cocktail lounge" and used the name "Tee Pee." The Tee Pee bar was the place to be during the annual Talkeetna Miner's Day celebration in July with live music and dancing. The couple divorced in 1991, and Al became the sole owner. During the 1990s, the Tee Pee hosted the Bachelor's Ball and Auction during the Talkeetna Winterfest in November, where local bachelors would "go on sale." During this time, the bar had a "Tee Pee Oasis" sign on the face of the building along with a plastic palm tree. In 2012, a routine visit by the Alcohol Beverage Control (ABC) board resulted in a violation because the name of the bar on the liquor license was the Talkeetna Motel. It was after this that Al wrote in the ABC required tourism statement that the bar has been "remodeled into a relaxing oasis for travelers w/rules not allowing foul language or upsetting behavior. This is not a bar." However, the motel stationary for 2018 used the names Talkeetna Motel, Alice's Kitchen, and Tee Pee Oasis Lounge.

In 2019, after almost 40 years of ownership, Al Sousa sold the business to William St. Pierre Jr. of Anchorage, and the name changed to the Talkeetna Inn. Al Sousa passed away in 2024.

☛**Visiting the Talkeetna Inn:** Their website declares that the name of the bar is "The Tavern" although it will undoubtably continue to be called the Tee Pee. Compared to the Fairview Inn, this is more the locals bar. The new owner has done a good job cleaning and modernizing the bar, and a game of pool is free.

From the Anchorage Daily News *– April 10, 1988.*

Longhorn Saloon
Mile 136 Denali Highway, Cantwell
(907) 768-2330

License issued: September 15, 1964, to Lloyd Davis (State Building & Investment Corp.)
Amenities: Pool table, darts, ping pong table, TV, food, occasional live music
Find them Online: Facebook (Cantwell Lodge – Longhorn Saloon)

History and Notoriety: In 1957, the small railroad town of Cantwell was finally linked to the Alaska road system with the completion of the Denali Highway. Lloyd Davis opened the Cantwell Bar in 1964 but changed the name to the Longhorn that same year. Ads from the 1970s show a photo of a Dall sheep with the horns of a Texas Longhorn Cow and the slogan "Home of the Longhorn Sheep."

William Sims and Jim Christopher bought the Longhorn in 1984. Christopher already owned much of Cantwell and had tried to "sell the town" in 1978. Bill and Sharon Sims, Keith Bulard and Glen Bailey became co-owners of the bar in 1990, and by 1993, Bulard and his wife Armeda were the sole owners.

In 2001, the *Anchorage Daily News* did a profile of Alaska State Trooper Sonny Sabala, who lived in Cantwell. One summer day, Sabala found a three-hundred-pound man in a dress sprawled across the road next to the Longhorn. The man, who had been drinking at the bar, was blocking traffic. A crowd from the bar watched as Sabal pried the man off the pavement and stuffed him into the back seat of the patrol car. The crowd started singing the theme song from the TV show *Cops*: 'Bad boys bad boys. Whatcha gonna do? Whatcha gonna do when they come for you." Sabala, from Texas, said later "It wasn't what I expected at all."

In 2006, scenes for the movie *Into the Wild* were filmed in and around Cantwell. Actor and movie director Sean Penn and his crew could be found at the Longhorn at the end of the day. Owner Armeda Bulard angrily gave Penn an earful after his pilot landed a plane on the lawn outside the bar one day.

☛**Visiting the Longhorn Saloon:** The bar is part of the Cantwell Lodge. Note the graffiti on the ceiling, typical of Alaskan bars. The Spring Rondy in April and the Bluegrass Festival in July are popular times to be at the Longhorn.

Fairbanks Daily News-Miner photo by Charles Darby

A new false front and gallons of paint failed to save the old Nevada bar in Fairbanks which since 1909 has been a home to some, a retreat to others, and a madhouse on Friday evenings. It was the first victim of the city's new building condemnation law and was closed during this past summer.

One of the last photos of the historic Nevada Bar in Fairbanks.
605 First Avenue, 1934 – 1971.
Alaska Magazine – October 1971

NOTORIOUS BARS OF INTERIOR ALASKA

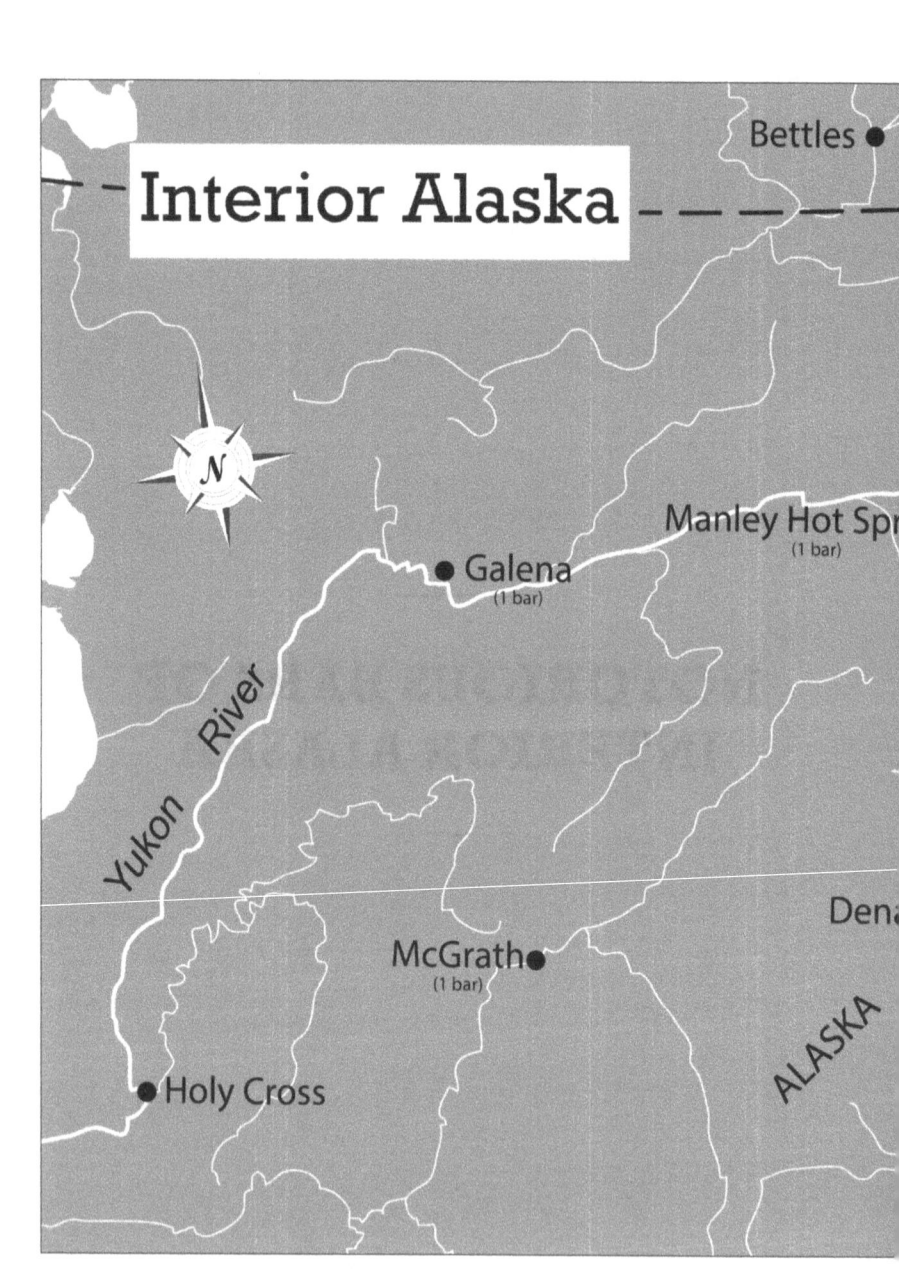

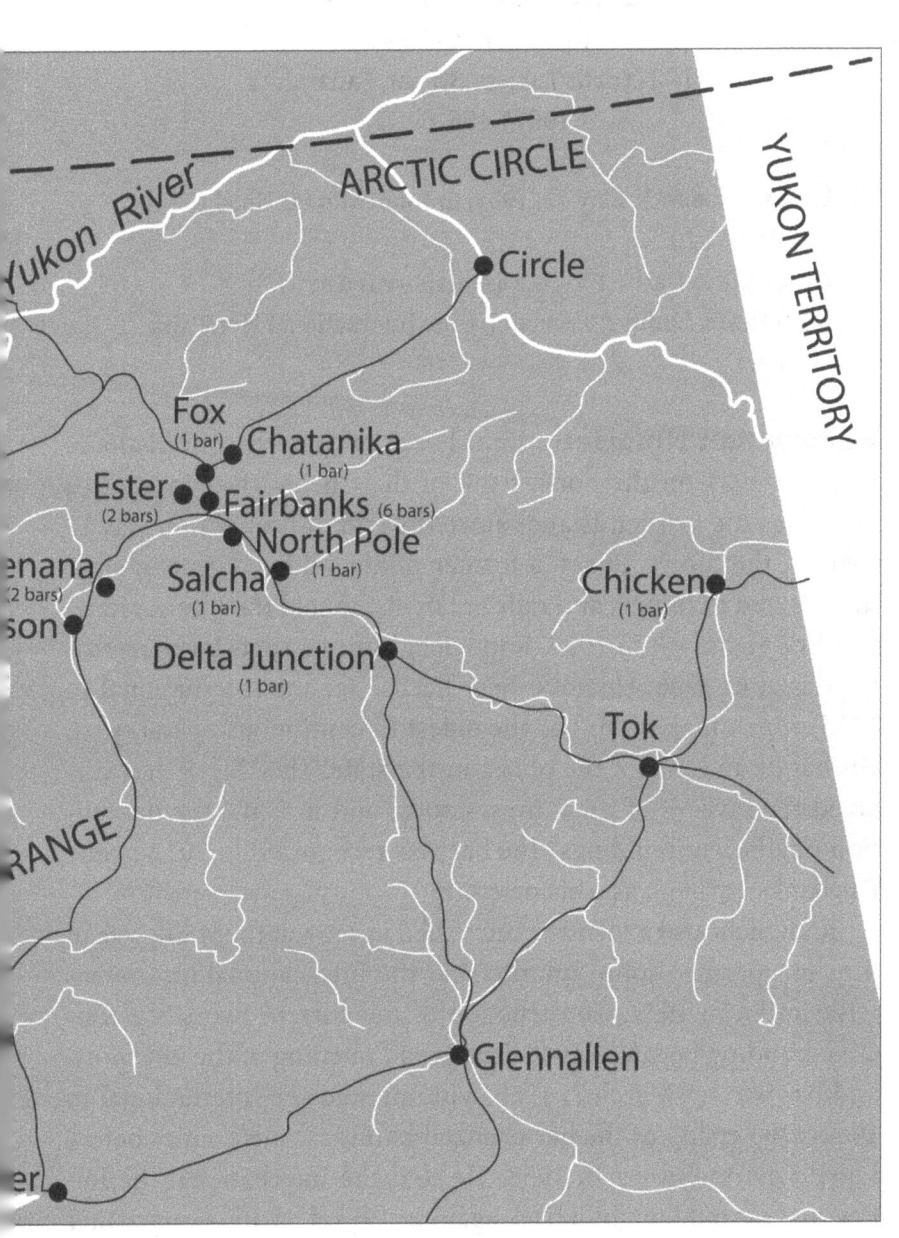

International Bar
(a.k.a. Big-I Pub)
122 North Turner Street, Fairbanks
(907) 456-6437

License issued: May 23, 1933, to International Hotel (Chris Radovich)
Amenities: Darts, TVs, occasional live music
Find them Online: Facebook (The International Hotel and Bar)

History and Notoriety: Emil Pozza opened the International Hotel in 1921 on the north bank of the Chena River in an area known as the Garden Island. Since the end of prohibition was 12 years in the future, Pozza, a former miner, added a general store that catered to miners and railroad men. He sold the International to Chris Radovich in 1927. Radovich, born in Yugoslavia, moved to Alaska in 1906. He got a beer license for the International in 1933, which makes this bar the oldest in continuous operation in Fairbanks and one of the oldest in the state. The "Big-I" has survived the ravages of time, fires, floods, and in 2009, the demolition of adjacent buildings. The bar was recognized in 2012 by the Fairbanks borough as a historic site.

Radovich, also a former miner, died in 1938 at the young age of fifty. His partner, John Vukmir, sold the International to Thomas Paskvan Sr. in 1939. Construction of the current two-story concrete building began in 1949. The grand opening of the new hotel and bar was on March 7, 1950. Vukmir sold the International in 1952. Ownership of the bar changed hands a couple times before Lloyd Levi took over in 1958. He sold the International the following year but bought it back again in 1961. Levi took on partner John "Jack" Sexton in 1963 and sold the bar to him in 1971. It was Sexton, from Minnesota, who projected his Irish heritage to the bar, an influence that is still evident today.

Sexton hired Bert "Hap" Ryder as manager in 1975. Ryder, from New Jersey, was an actor and local teacher of performing arts, and a fixture of the Big-I until his death in 2007. The Hap Ryder Riverfront Theatre is named in his honor. Sexton sold the Big-I to John Jackovich in 2006 and passed away in 2009. Jackovich sold the bar to Nathan Davis in 2020. Davis died three years later at the early age of 44.

In the summer of 1974, George W. Bush lived and worked in Fairbanks. In a 2000 article in the *New York Times*, Sally Smith, a Democrat and future mayor of Juneau who was also living in Fairbanks that summer, said she went out with the future president several times. "We went to the International Bar, kind of a hangout for people in the arts and people who write for the newspaper," she said. "I remember we had a beer. That's all I remember."

☛**Visiting the International Bar**: The Big-I celebrates its history with a wall of photos of former patrons. A sign from the notorious Nevada Bar is here, as Sexton was the last owner. A tradition of strictly female bartenders began during the pipeline days. The St. Patrick's Day celebration on the Sunday closest to March 17 is legendary and is a not-to-be-missed party.

From Lou Jacobin's Guide to Alaska and the Yukon – 1954.

Mecca Bar
549 Second Avenue, Fairbanks
(907) 456-6320

License issued: June 1945 to Roy F. Snyder and Joe E. Mainella
Amenities: Pool table, occasional live music
Find them Online: Facebook

History and Notoriety: In 1940, Roy Snyder opened the Mecca Bar in Kodiak. The bar was such a success that in 1945, Snyder decided to open another bar, this time in Fairbanks, which is over five hundred miles from Kodiak. Snyder and his partner Joe Mainella bought the Reception Bar and changed the name to the Mecca Bar. Later that year, the distinctive neon marquee sign was installed out front, which Snyder and Mainella said signified "A Sign of Good Times." Snyder hired Tommy Jones, his best bartender from Kodiak, and C.R. "Joe" Smith as managers.

In 1952, Roy decided to focus on the Mecca Bar in Kodiak. By 1957, Mainella had also moved on, and Joe Smith had partnered with Wallace "Wally" Burnett Jr., who took control of the Mecca in 1959. Burnett later became a city councilman and sold the bar to his brother Donald "Deke" Burnett in 1970. In the book *Last Call!* bartender Judy Thompson told author Richard Robinson about her ten years working for the Burnett brothers. She described Wally as a "crusty old guy" with a generous streak, and Deke as being "so cute" when he referred to himself as a "drunk [expletive deleted] cowboy." Deke sold the bar in 1989, ending a thirty-two-year Burnett legacy.

In the early 1950s, the downstairs portion of the bar was called the Sports Mecca. By 1956, it had been transformed into a café presided over by Chef Jimmy Lee. Joe Vogler, a politician who founded the Alaska Independence Party, met and proposed to his future wife Doris in the cafe. The café became the Tiki Cove restaurant in 1962, serving Chinese food. In 1971, Deke found two men hiding there after business hours. They were arrested and indicted on burglary charges. After a flood, Tiki Cove moved to the Polaris Building in 1977, and the days of the Mecca having a restaurant in the basement ended. The resident ghost in the basement is presumed to be Deke.

The Mecca was extremely popular during the pipeline construction years. At that time, the Fairbanks Bar, the Flame Lounge, and the Arctic Bar were across the street, the Cottage Bar a few doors down, and the Savoy, Tommy's Elbow Room, Polaris, and Cabaret on the next block. Alas, the Mecca is the lone survivor of the once notorious "Two Street" bars.

In 2024, the Fairbanks City Council voted 4-1 to protest the Mecca's license renewal because of public safety and vandalism concerns. The protest sparked a community rally of supporters for the Mecca and its owner, Jodi Blakley. A move for reconsideration resulted in a 6-0 vote to approve the license renewal.

☛Visiting the Mecca Bar: The booths along the wall are long gone but much of the Mecca has remained intact. Owner Jodi Blakley has done a wonderful job repairing and maintaining many of the original fixtures, including giving the marquee sign a makeover. The Yukon Quest and North American sled dog races begin on Second Avenue directly in front of the Mecca. The bar is also very popular during the summer solstice and during the Golden Days celebration in July.

Sports Mecca Bar Fairbanks, Alaska J. E. Mainella
Sports Mecca Cafe   R. F. Snyder

*Mecca postcard – circa 1950.
Courtesy of Patricia De Nardo Schmidt*

Midnite Mine
(a.k.a. The Mine)
308 Wendell Avenue, Fairbanks
(907) 456-5348

License Issued: November 28, 1971, to Larry K. Wike
Amenities: Pool table, darts, foosball, TV's, jukebox.
Find them Online: Facebook

History and Notoriety: By the time Larry Wike opened the Midnite Mine, he had already owned the Clear Sky Lodge in Clear, and the Riverside and Wonder bars in Fairbanks. Wike, born in 1935 in North Carolina, knew that the oil boom was going to bring a lot of thirsty men to town and that another bar would be a good investment. He would soon own the Howling Dog in Ester (now in Fox) and the Badger Den in North Pole.

In 1972, John Kirkley and Bob Maloney became partners with Wike. It was Maloney who built the fireplace, which is now almost hidden by bras, trophies, and paraphernalia. Maloney had a dog named Jazz—a frequent visitor to the bar in the 1980s. Jazz was taught to associate money with dog treats and would nose into the purses of female customers looking for cash. According to a bartender (from the book *Last Call!* by Richard Robinson) Jazz could distinguish between real and fake money. He would take paper money, credit cards, and even personal checks, but had no interest in Monopoly money or any other imitation currency. The dog even took a sealed cigarette case that had cash folded inside it. All attempts to trick Jazz were futile.

In 2008, a man came into the crowded bar and shot his ex-girlfriend's new boyfriend. The victim survived four bullet wounds but is now a quadriplegic. The assailant was sentenced to seventy years in prison.

Wike passed away in 2014, and Maloney sold the bar to Rick Mensik in 2017. In 2019, the Midnite Mine Brewing Company opened on the first floor above the bar.

> **☛Visiting the Midnite Mine:** Walking down the stairs into the bar is like descending into an actual mine. The ceiling is black and there are rocks on the walls, which are supported by large timbers. Add in the rock waterfall and graffiti, and the resemblance is convincing. The outdoor deck is a great alternative on a summer day. The bar is open 365 days a year but doesn't open until 6 PM Christmas Day.

The Boatel
3368 Riverside Drive, Fairbanks
(907) 479-6537

License Issued: 1961 to Clifford R. Everts and Noel E. Kennon
Amenities: Pool table, darts, TVs, horseshoes, occasional live music
Find them Online: Facebook

History and Notoriety: In 1956, the sternwheeler *Yukon Health*, which had carried medical services to villages along the Tanana and Yukon rivers, was retired from service. It was towed to Fairbanks and docked on the Chena River. The boat was refurbished into the *Riviera Boatel* in 1958, with staterooms for just five dollars a night. Cliff Everts, born in New York, came to Alaska in 1943 and was a pilot with Wien Alaska Airlines. Everts bought the Boatel in 1960, and he and partner Noel Kennon acquired a liquor license the following year. The grand opening of the cocktail lounge was July 15, 1961. By 1964, it was known simply as The Boatel.

During the 1960s, the Boatel became more of a restaurant and night spot than a hotel, advertising live music and occasionally exotic dancers. Fire destroyed the Boatel in the early morning hours of May 26, 1970. Arson was suspected as an empty gas can was found nearby. The Boatel was rebuilt in the same location as a simple rectangular structure overlooking the Chena.

From 1971 – 1976, the bar sponsored the Boatel Cup Race, a short course involving three heats with six laps each. Spectators sat on the deck of the bar and observed the fast and not-so-fast vessels (i.e., converted bathtubs).

Jon Neubauer, born in Seattle but raised in Alaska, became a partner with Everts in 1971. The Neubauer family took full control in 1986 and still owns the bar today. Jon Neubauer passed away in 2003, and people still talk about the wake that was held at the Boatel.

Larry "Hack" Hackenmiller, former owner of the Club Manchu (now closed) once worked as a bartender at the Boatel. In the book *Last Call!* Hackenmiller told author Robinson two great stories about his time here. A female tourist requested a blended margarita and was told that the Boatel didn't have a blender. When she pointed to a blender behind the bar, the bartender grabbed the device and threw it into the river. Another time a young woman came into the bar wearing a hospital gown and confessed that she was from the mental ward of the Fairbanks hospital. Hack told her "Well you came to the right bar. Let's have a drink." Hack passed away in 2022.

In March 2007, the movie *Chronic Town* was filmed in Fairbanks. The primary character, Truman, is a foul-mouthed, drugged-out cab driver who loses his girlfriend and, after a binge at the Boatel (filmed on location), winds up in a mental hospital. The film received positive reviews after being shown at the Sundance and Anchorage international film festivals in 2008. Natalie Neubauer, a real-life employee of the Boatel, played a waitress at the bar.

☛**Visiting the Boatel:** This "sleazy waterfront bar" is a Fairbanks institution that is proud of its history. Check out the photos and great souvenirs. The deck is a wonderful place for river travelers to take a break during the summer months, and the lawn has a stage for concerts. The Boatel celebrates all the holidays, as well as the bar's birthday.

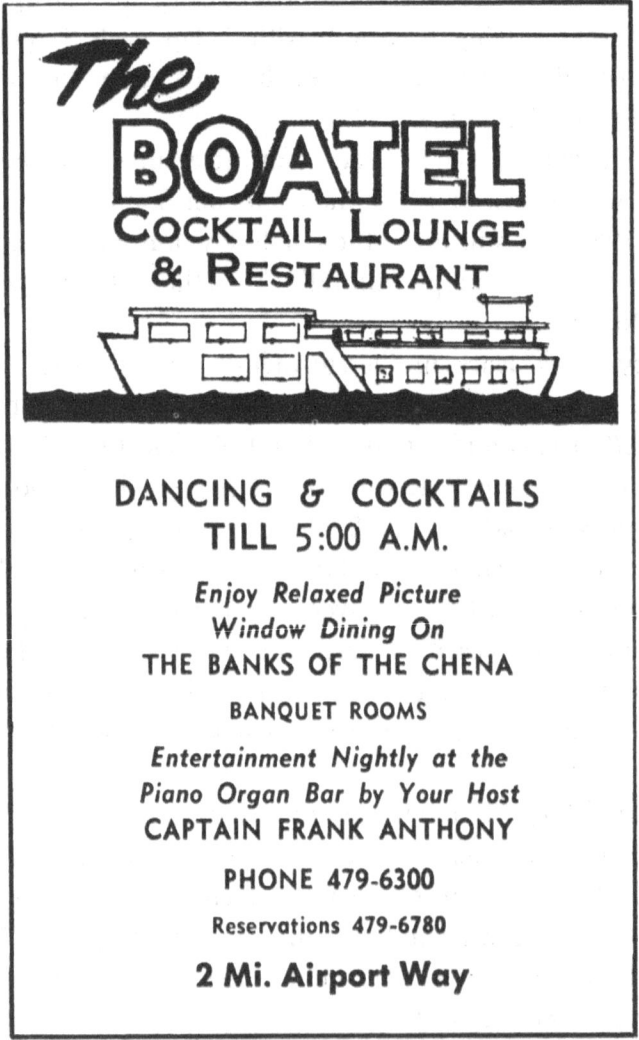

From Alaska Travel Guide, *Editor: Larry Lake – 1967.*

Golden Eagle Saloon
3630 Main Street, Ester
(907) 479-0809

License Issued: 1982 to Eugene III and Patricia Reed
Amenities: Pool table, darts, TVs, occasional live music
Find them Online: Facebook

History and Notoriety: In 1908, the Golden Eagle Hotel in Ester advertised "First Class Rooms" and a "Fine Pool Room and Bar." It did not survive prohibition, but the new Golden Eagle wears the old name with pride.

This bar began as the Gold Bucket in 1965 in a building that was once Bertha Moody's store. It became the Howling Dog Inn in 1968. Owner Chip Trainor described the building as "a real dog. I knew it was going to howl." Larry Wike, who owned the Midnite Mine in Fairbanks, bought the bar in 1972. Mike Gordon, who owned Chilkoot Charlie's in Anchorage, bought it in 1976 and changed the name to Chilkoot Charlie's. One year later, Wike bought it back and renamed it the Red Garter Saloon. Eugene and Patricia Reed bought it in 1980, renaming it the Golden Eagle in 1982. The rightful name had finally returned to this Ester institution. The old building was torn down and a new one built with the old lumber.

Dan O'Neill, an author from Fairbanks, described the Howling Dog Inn in an article in the *Fairbanks Daily News-Miner* about a local band called the Glass Bead Game. "The old Howling Dog in Ester, with its sawdust floor, sunken bar, and upstairs gallery. Pretty girls dancing in bunny boots, their long hair flying. Guys looking like gold rush miners. Their long hair flying. And everyone smelling (sic) of creosote and beer and pot (which was legal). If you think this is sheer nostalgic reverie, you are right. I miss those times. I think they were better."

The Golden Eagle is called the "living room of Ester." The bar is the biggest business in town and the parking area is the Ester town square. An annual event in Ester is the LiBerry Music Fest and Pie Throwdown, held in September. This festival is usually held at the Golden Eagle and the music, food, and flow of libations make this a not-to-be-missed party.

☞**Visiting the Golden Eagle Saloon:** Other popular times to be at the Golden Eagle are Independence Day and New Years Eve. The Golden Eagle is a cash only bar.

Mrs. Bertha Moody's Store, now the Golden Eagle Saloon. From William Tewkesbury's Guide to Alaska – 1950

Skinny Dick's Halfway Inn
8910 (Mile 327.9) Parks Highway, Ester
(907) 388-5770

License Issued: April 26, 1982, to Richard Hiland and Wayne and Sally Taylor
Amenities: Pool table, darts, TVs
Find them Online: https://skinnydicks.net/; Facebook

History and Notoriety: This famous bar began as the Halfway House, so named because it's located about halfway between Fairbanks and Nenana. Donald and Karole Deck converted an old sawmill barracks into the bar, which opened in 1968.

Richard Hiland was born in Milwaukee in 1928 and moved to Fairbanks in 1969 after a nasty divorce. He worked as a bartender in Clear where he picked up his nickname "Skinny Dick." The man was truly skinny; so skinny that he wore a women's style watch because he said, "If I put a men's watch on, it'll look like an alarm clock."

In 1981, Hiland and his partners Wayne and Sally Taylor bought the Halfway House, renaming it in 1982. By 1985, he was the sole owner. Hiland decided to capitalize on the sexual connation of the bar's name and purchased shirts, pins, hats, coats, panties, and condoms, all with the name of the bar and some with a drawing of mating polar bears. Travelers, particularly tourists, took notice and purchased his souvenirs. The bar caught the attention of Mr. Whitekeys, owner of Anchorage's Fly-By-Night Club and creator of the *Whale Fat Follies* comedy revue. Whitekeys (real name Douglas Haggar) not only informed the audience about the bar but made the chant 'Skinnnnny Dick's Half-Way Inn!' a regular part of the show.

I, like so many other Alaskans, first learned of the bar from the *Whale Fat Follies*. My wife and I had the privilege of being served by Hiland when we eventually visited. He nodded his approval when we ordered shots of tequila. Hiland liked to tell the story of how he got his first DUI. When he was pulled over, he fell on the ground as he stepped out of his car. The police officer told him to "Jump up and down on one foot." Hiland replied "I can't do that sober." Hiland finished the story by saying "Boy, I was in handcuffs so fast. It took 'em 61 years to catch me." The colorful Skinny Dick Hiland passed away in 2008.

☞**Visiting Skinny Dick's:** Even though Hiland is no longer with us, his bar is still here and more than worth the visit. You must love a bar that warns you "Enter at your own risk" before you even get inside. Buy a souvenir and try not to open or use it; it will be a collector's item someday. The bar is open only mid-April through October, but souvenirs are always available on the website.

Richard "Skinny Dick" Hiland (1928 – 2008).

Monroe's Monderosa
(a.k.a. The Mondo)
Mile 309 Parks Highway, Nenana
(907) 832-5243

License Issued: February 23, 1982, to Nicholas and Carol Monroe
Amenities: Pool table, TVs, food, liquor store
Find them Online: Facebook (Monderosa)

History and Notoriety: Back in 1968, there was a restaurant and bar here called Parker's Patch Lodge, which burned to the ground in 1981. Nick Monroe, born in 1949 and raised in Nenana, bought the property and had a new bar and restaurant constructed out of white spruce logs. The name is a combination of his last name and Ponderosa, after the name of the ranch on the old TV western *Bonanza*.

The Monderosa is easy to find because of the Department of Transportation signs announcing the turn-off to the bar. This is one of the very few Alaskan bars with such a distinction. It is famous for its "Mondo" hamburgers, which are exceptionally large, especially the "Monstrosity Monster" with a one-pound patty.

In 2006, a man who was jealous of an ex-girlfriend started a fistfight in the Monderosa. The fight spilled outside the bar and a third man got involved who was stabbed and later died. According to witnesses, as many as thirty people were fighting or watching the brawl. The murder trial resulted first in a mistrial and later a verdict of not guilty for the accused.

Monroe was an accomplished guitar player and singer who had a love for Elvis Presley. He enjoyed entertaining at the Mondo and was easily recognizable by his mustache. He passed away in 2019 and his wife Donna Mather now owns the bar.

☛**Visiting Monroe's Monderosa:** The building might remind some folks of *Bonanza* except for the small shrine to Elvis Presley behind the bar. Hamburgers and Bloody Mary's are always good choices here. The Monderosa is a cash only bar.

Nick Monroe (1949 - 2019).
Photo courtesy of Donna Mather

Moochers Bar
814 A Street (Corner of Front and A Streets), Nenana
(907) 832-5402

License Issued: 1952 to George and Fred Hupprich
Amenities: Pool table, darts, TVs, occasional live music, liquor store
Find them Online: Facebook

History and Notoriety: Moochers was once known as the Alibi Club, located here in 1948. According to former owner Vern Weiss, the name "moochers" refers to young local women who would come to this bar to flirt and mooch drinks from the men who worked for the Alaska Railroad.

George Hupprich, from Oregon, moved to Nenana in 1911 and had worked as a longshoreman for the railroad. He and his son Fred still owned Moochers in 1955 when it was damaged by a fire that destroyed the Corner Bar (later rebuilt). In 1956, new owner Donald Cook was shot and killed by a man as he stepped outside the front door of the bar. The man was tried and sentenced to life in prison in 1958 but was later paroled. Bob and May Speck bought the bar shortly after the murder and owned it for almost 20 years.

Weiss, born in 1932 in Illinois, bought Moochers in 1976. He had worked on the trans-Alaska oil pipeline as a welder and had friends who worked on the barges going up and down the Tanana River. They supplied him with the tugboat bell and the orange lifesavers that hang on the walls of the bar. Weiss was civic-minded and was instrumental in securing the grant that brought Railbelt Mental Health services to Nenana. He passed away in 2015 and his wife Carolene owned the bar until 2017.

Moochers is known to most Alaskans as the bar most closely associated with the Nenana Ice Classic, the most famous ice sweepstakes (lottery) in the world. Wagering on the exact time that the ice will break up in the spring on the Tanana River has been a tradition since 1917. Moochers is just around the corner from the tripod, which has made the bar the unofficial headquarters for spectators of this slow-motion contest.

☛**Visiting Moochers:** This is another Alaskan bar that honors its past patrons by hanging their framed photos on the wall. Tripod Days in March and Independence Day, when motorcycle clubs descend on the town, are popular times to be at Moochers.

Vern Weiss (1932 – 2015).
From the Fairbanks Daily News-Miner *– July 14, 2015*

Clear Sky Lodge
Mile 280 Parks Highway, Anderson
(907) 582-2251

License Issued: 1961 to William Roberts, Larry Wike, Douglas Jones, and Theresa Bessette
Amenities: Pool table, darts, cornhole, TVs, food, occasional live music, liquor store
Find them Online: Facebook

History and Notoriety: In 1960, construction began on a huge missile-detecting radar site near a station known as Clear on the Alaska Railroad. In June of that year, William "Bill" Roberts met with the ABC Board and described his plans for building a motel and a bar close to the facility on the new "McKinley Park Highway." Senator John Coghill from Nenana endorsed the plans and in October 1961, Roberts and his partner Larry Wike announced the opening of the Clear Sky Lodge, which began as a bar in a log building with a gas station. Grand opening was November 11.

Both Roberts and Wike were pilots, and they decided to build a twenty-five-hundred-foot landing strip directly behind the bar. The Clear Sky Lodge airport is today an FAA recognized airstrip. Wike bought Roberts's share of the bar in 1964 and then bought the Riverside and Wonder bars in Fairbanks. Wike sold the Clear Sky Lodge to Gary Smith and Bruce Harden in 1967. The partners ran ads that encouraged customers to "relax beside our cozy fireplace." Harden became the sole owner in 1972, and the lodge hosted shooting matches for sportsmen who used black powder muzzle loaders. Carol and Fred Shields bought the lodge in 1983 and sold it to Sandee and Don Rabideau in 2004.

In 2008, the lodge made national news when a black bear sow tried walking in the front door, which prompted the bartender to shoot it. No zoos would take her two cubs, so they were exterminated shortly after.

Matt and Vicki Nelson bought the lodge in 2019. The lodge celebrated its sixtieth-year anniversary in 2021.

☞**Visiting the Clear Sky Lodge**: The original log building is still here, and so is the antique piano and the huge log beams that are inscribed with the names of long-ago customers. The bar serves a great steak dinner, and the outdoor beer garden has a play set for kids.

From the Fairbanks Daily News-Miner – *November 8, 1961.*

Badger Den
(a.k.a. The Den)
1447 Old Badger Road, North Pole
(907) 488-6757

License Issued: October 10, 1978, to John Manley, John Kirkley, and Larry Wike

Amenities: Pool table, darts, horseshoes, TVs, food, occasional live music

Find them Online: Facebook

History and Notoriety: The name Badger comes from Harry M. Badger (1869 – 1965) who had a farm along the road now bearing his name. In the 1950s and '60s, a bar named the Badgers Den was located on Badger Road just 500 feet from the Badger Gate into Ladd Army Airfield (now Fort Wainwright). While that bar didn't last, the Badger Den on Old Badger Road has become a local favorite and a destination for bikers.

The bar initially got a cold reception from the neighborhood. Larry Wike (who also owned the Midnite Mine bar in Fairbanks and the Howling Dog in Ester) and his partners first applied for a liquor license in May of 1976. A group of locals filed an injunction, claiming that the business would cause, among other things, injury to their children and lower property values. The case stalled the opening of the bar for two years. In 1985, Wike took full ownership of the bar.

Last paragraph, first sentence. Larry "Hack" Hackenmiller, former owner of the Club Manchu (now closed) in Fairbanks, claimed to be the first bartender hired at the Badger Den. In the book *Last Call!* Hack described how he would entertain customers by hitting bottles with a pair of spoons in time to the theme song from the *Lone Ranger* TV show. Other songs he chimed were *Thank God I'm A Country Boy*, and *There Is No Beer In Heaven*. Hack passed away in 2022.

☛**Visiting the Badger Den**: Patrons are encouraged to grill your own steaks here. The bar can be packed on Memorial Day, Independence Day, and Labor Day.

Boon Dox Bar
(a.k.a. Boondox Bar; a.k.a. Riverside Bar)
7271 Richardson Highway, Salcha
(907) 385-6636

License Issued: 1957 to Gerald "Jerry" and Gertrude "Boots" King
Amenities: Pool table, TV, food
Find them Online: Facebook (Riverside Bar)

History and Notoriety: The community along the Richardson Highway known as Salcha was very much like being in the boondocks back when Jerry and Boots decided to open a bar and liquor store here. The Richardson Highway had just been paved, and the couple chose a beautiful spot adjacent to the Tanana River. However, this area of the river is prone to flooding, sometimes due to ice jams. Newspaper articles in the 2000s reporting on the floods occasionally referred to an ice jam as the "Boondox Bar ice jam."

In 1961, the King' sold the bar to George and Amelia "Toby" Couture. George passed away in 1969, and Toby sold the bar to William Harvey. She missed the Boon Dox as she bought it back in 1971. Along with Thomas and Harriet Ganley, she would continue to own the bar for the next ten years. Ads from the 1970s invited folks to visit the bar on Sundays for a free smorgasbord and live music. Toby sold the bar to Anne Burnett in 1981. Anne was the wife of Donald "Deke" Burnett, who with his brother Wally owned the notorious Mecca Bar in Fairbanks.

Unfortunately, the 1990s were a tough decade for the bar. In 1992, a man walked out of the bar, lied down on the highway, and was struck and killed by a car. In 1997, a man who had been drinking at the bar drove his car into another vehicle resulting in three deaths, including his own. As a result, one of the bartenders was charged with over-service (later dismissed), a second bartender was charged with not having an alcohol server card, and the owner was charged with knowingly allowing the unlicensed bartender to serve drinks. In 1998, a fire destroyed the bar. Locals called for help, but no fire department would respond, as it was not a life-threatening emergency. The bar was rebuilt in 1999, and Michael Stormont bought the new Boon Dox Bar in 2002. Stormont died and in 2021, and ownership passed to his son Clyde.

> ☛**Visiting the Boon Dox Bar:** While the historic charm of the old Boon Dox bar is gone, the new bar is still in the same picturesque location.

NOW OPEN . . .
Jerry & Boots King's
Boondox Bar

Open Daily Noon to Midnite

33 Short Miles on the Richardson.

First ad. Fairbanks Daily News-Miner – April 19, 1958.

Trophy Lodge
Mile 1420 Alaska Highway, Delta Junction
(907) 895-4685

License Name Change Issued: 1956 to Carl and Geneva Revord
Amenities: TVs, food, occasional live entertainment
Find them Online: https://www.trophylodgeak.com/; Facebook

History and Notoriety: Carl and Geneva "Jean" Revord, civilian employees at Fort Greely, opened the Rancho Delta Bar at this location in 1954. In 1956, they changed the name to the Trophy Lodge and lined the walls of the bar with pelts and heads of Alaskan game: sheep, moose, caribou, bear, lynx, and red fox were some of the first. The bar soon featured lodging, a dining room with a grand piano, and live entertainment. In 1964, the "Beetles" appeared (local boys who pantomimed the Fab Four) and reportedly had the ladies screaming and fainting.

In 1974, "streaking" (running naked through a public place) was the rage in the United States, and two local girls decided to be the first to streak when the temperature was negative forty degrees Fahrenheit. The *Fairbanks Daily News Miner* reported they ran through several Delta area bars, including the Trophy. All the bar owners—and patrons—thought the stunt was great, except for June Hooks, who had bought the Trophy in 1972. Her letter to the editor of the *News Miner* complained about the "indecent exposure" and pointed out that "coats were held for them at doors, and they ran through heated buildings." Despite the ski masks they were wearing, most people were able to figure out who the girls were.

Erika Elledge and Sigurd and Lys Bergstad bought the bar in 1976. They sold it to Albert Gartz and Edward Clemens in 1987. Randy Wood bought the bar in 1988 and owned it until 2022, selling it to Tim Clark.

Windstorms during the winter of 1999 – 2000 significantly damaged the Trophy Lodge and forced the demolition of the original building. It was rebuilt and continues to be popular with pipeline workers, the hunting and fishing crowd, and the locals.

> **Visiting the Trophy Lodge:** A few of the trophies are still on the walls, but the atmosphere has changed due to the new building. The multiple TVs and professional football jerseys in glass cases give it a sports bar feel.

Chicken Creek Saloon
No. 1 Airport Road, Chicken
(907) 388-2904 (café)

License Issued: August 29, 1978, to David and Susan McCall
Amenities: Pool table, occasional live music, liquor store
Find them Online: https://chickenalaska.com/; Facebook

History and Notoriety: This is the only bar in the world named Chicken. This has been a gold mining area since 1895, and mining remains the primary industry today.

The building that houses the saloon (and the rest of "downtown") was built as a hotel in 1975. David and Susan McCall managed a store in Eagle before moving to Chicken and opening the saloon. The bar had a reputation as a rough and rowdy place when Greg and Susan Wiren, from New Jersey, bought property in Chicken in 1988, including the saloon. Susan Wiren told author Harry Walker for his book *Wacky and Wonderful Roadside Attractions of Alaska* "I was afraid to walk into the place. I cleaned out the rowdies."

The Chicken Creek Saloon has a cannon, known as the "panty cannon." The cannon (an iron tube) is loaded with underwear, or toilet paper, and then fired. The ritual involves a customer voluntarily handing over their underwear. The underwear is blasted out of the cannon into the street, and the remaining shreds stapled to the ceiling of the bar. According to bartender Amy Cunningham, some customers will perform a strip tease, making this unusual tradition even more hilarious.

Chicken was designated as a Historic District and placed on the National Register of Historic Places on September 30, 2001.

☛**Visiting the Chicken Creek Saloon:** All kinds of chicken souvenirs can be bought here, including the classic t-shirt "I was laid in Chicken Alaska." The Chickenstock musical celebration in June is a great reason to journey to Chicken and visit the saloon. The bar is only open from May 15 to September 15.

Howling Dog Saloon
(a.k.a. The Dog)
2160 Old Steese Highway North, Fox
(907) 456-4695

License Issued: July 9, 1976, to N and S Corporation
Amenities: Pool tables, darts, foosball, volleyball, food, occasional live music
Find them Online: https://www.howlingdogsaloonak.com/; Facebook

History and Notoriety: In 1975, Larry Wike opened the Gateway Motel and Bar in a building that once housed the Fox General Store. Wike also owned the Howling Dog Inn in Ester, which had become a nuisance to the Esterites (parking problems, loud music). Wike sold it and took the bar's name with him. He and his new partners Joe Nyquist and Jim Smith (N and S) agreed that Howling Dog was a better name for a bar than the Gateway. In 1977, Nyquist became the sole owner and in 1979 Mike Brock became a partner. Brock had worked on construction of the trans-Alaska oil pipeline and had been a bouncer at the bar, and it was he that added the word saloon to the bar's name. Country music was popular at the bar in the 1970s. Rock and blues took over in the '80s and remained the standard.

Anna Farneski wrote a profile on the Howling Dog for the *Fairbanks Daily News Miner* in 1988. She described the décor: "The walls of the bar, with its low ceiling, are crammed with memorabilia given to Brock by customers: out-of-state license plates left by newly arrived Alaskans, an antique typewriter, a bearskin with a plywood plaque saying 'shot on the Howling Dog dance floor,' and antlers from a customer's first and only moose." Also noted was an entire wall covered with photos of customers past and present, how many of the chairs are gouged with graffiti, and that a red carpet which was used to welcome Pope John Paul II and President Reagan to Fairbanks in 1984 covers the stage. Many of these items remain in the bar to this day.

From 1994 to 2016, the bar was the home of "Foodstock" which was an annual three-day outdoor music festival held during summer solstice that collected food and cash for the needy. More recently, the Dog sponsored the Mr. Facejacket beard contest, with money raised going to the Fairbanks Food Bank. Ralph Glasgow, who has owned the Dog since 2003, schedules live music every weekend.

☛Visiting the Howling Dog Saloon: Be sure to walk around and check out the decorations. Cinco de Mayo and Halloween are big celebrations. The Howling Dog is a seasonal bar, which means it's usually closed from November through April.

Chatanika Lodge
5760 (Mile 29) Steese Highway, Chatanika
(907) 389-2164

License Issued: January 17, 1958, to Otto Bubenicek
Amenities: Pool table, foosball, pinball, TV, food, occasional live music, liquor store
Find them Online: Facebook

History and Notoriety: This bar has its roots in the Chatanika Trading Post, located in "Old" Chatanika one mile southwest of the current lodge. Robert Sr. "Bob" and Frances Cacy bought the store in 1923 and sold retail liquor in 1934. In the late 1930s, Old Chatanika was dredged for the gold beneath its streets. Helen Cacy (daughter of Bob and Frances) and her husband Everett "Pat" Patton moved the trading post to the current location.

Otto and Edith Bubenicek bought the trading post in 1948. Otto Bubenicek, born in New Jersey and raised in Austria, was an experienced carpenter, butcher, and cook. In 1958, he obtained a Roadhouse dispensary license and opened the bar. By 1962, locals referred to the business as the Chatanika Lodge. In 1969, Bubenicek sold the lodge to Warren "Bud" and Mary Fyten.

Terry and Ron Franklin, brothers from Iowa, bought the lodge in 1974. Terry owned three bars in Fairbanks and testified in court that same year after witnessing a murder at the Cottage Bar. The lodge burned to the ground in 1975. According to Ron Franklin's wife Shirley in the book *Last Call!* Ron dragged an empty barn to the burn site and reopened the bar. The lodge was expanded, and a restaurant was added in 1988. Terry Franklin passed away in 2000.

From 1979 – 2010, the lodge held Outhouse Races in March. The highly decorated outhouses were carried by teams of five, who propelled them over a one-mile course on snow and ice. Most of the outhouses were on skis, but some on go-cart frames.

The lodge was used as an evacuation shelter during the "Boundary Fire" in July 2004, until the fire got too close. Ron vowed not to leave but had all the photos, guns, furs, and mining memorabilia taken off the walls and packed up just in case. He later parked a 1955 Ford Thunderbird and two Harley Davidson motorcycles inside the bar. Ron Franklin passed away in 2023.

Unique to this bar is what has been described as Christmas kitsch, with some thirty thousand multi-colored lights that stay lit all year, tinsel, garlands, and plastic Santas.

☛**Visiting the Chatanika Lodge:** Annual traditions include the Chatanika Lodge Car and Bike Show in August. Independence Day, Halloween, Christmas, and New Years Eve are also popular times to be here.

*Ron Franklin (1947 – 2023).
Photo courtesy of Shirley Franklin*

Manley Roadhouse
(a.k.a. Manley Lodge)
100 Front Street, Manley Hot Springs
(907) 672-3161

License Issued: 1958 to Gilbert Monroe
Amenities: Pool table, TV, food, occasional live music
Find them Online: https://www.manleylodge.com/; Facebook

History and Notoriety: The Manley Roadhouse was built in 1903 when this area was known simply as Hot Springs. Daniel and Elsie Green were the owners in 1930 and 1940, and Lloyd and Jean Hubbard in 1955. Hot Springs was renamed Manley Hot Springs in 1957. The new owner Gilbert Monroe, from Fairbanks, changed the name to Manley Lodge and opened the bar. In 1959, the Elliott Highway opened, connecting Manley Hot Springs with Fairbanks.

Cyril and Margaret "Daisy" Hetherington became the owners in 1964 and changed the name to the Black Bear Lodge. Daisy Hetherington, who worked for the *Fairbanks Daily News Miner*, reported that the bar was used as a church for Christmas service that year. In 1965, Lewis and Phyliss Beyer, Bill Fuller, and Stanley Robertson bought it and changed the name back to the Manley Lodge. By 1968, Lewis Beyer was the sole owner and later that year sold the lodge to Harlan and Dora Hohman. The couple sold it in 1970 to Robert E. (Bob) Lee, Jr.

Lee, from Minnesota, moved to Alaska in 1965 and worked as a State Trooper in Fairbanks. He fell in love with Manley Hot Springs, became postmaster, and bought the Trading Post in 1979.

In May of 1984, a lone and disturbed drifter killed at least six people near the Manley boat launch on the Tanana River. At the very time when the murders occurred, Lee was driving to the launch to look for a stove fitting at an old fish plant. Fate intervened and a friend waved him down, saying he had just what Lee needed. He returned to the roadhouse with the fitting, an action he realized later probably saved his life. Lee kept the fitting on top of the stove in the bar for years.

Lee married Lisa Lee Owens in a ceremony at the Manley Roadhouse in 2007, and together they managed the business until he passed away in 2009. Sukakpak, Inc. bought the Roadhouse from Lisa Lee Owens in 2023.

➤**Visiting the Manley Roadhouse:** This historic roadhouse was remodeled in 2024. The bar itself is U-shaped and is a great place to hang out and meet the locals. Independence Day is celebrated at Manley Hot Springs with a parade and fish derby.

Yukon Inn
(a.k.a. Hobo's; a.k.a. Archie's)
169 River Front Drive, Galena
(907) 656-1285

License Issued: 1959 to Frank Benson and Norman Burgett
Amenities: Pool table, darts, TV, food, occasional live music
Find them Online: Facebook

History and Notoriety: The Yukon Inn is one of just three bars in Alaska that have had a book written about it (the Alaskan in Juneau and the Salty Dawg in Homer are the other two). *The Untold Story of Hobo and Dangerous Dan McGrew* by Ken Lavigne describes the early days of the bar and the beautiful illustrations that once decorated its walls.

Frank "Hobo" Benson, born 1924 in Michigan, moved to Anchorage in 1948 where he opened a plumbing and heating business. He expanded into bar equipment and in 1959 came to Galena and met Norman "Buckets" Burgett. The two hit it off and decided to open the Yukon Inn, where guests could eat, sleep, and get a good drink. On December 1, 1959, William A. "Bill" Egan, the first Governor of the State, spent the first dollar there.

In 1962, Benson met artist Yvonne Worthington in Anchorage. She wanted to visit remote areas of Alaska, and Benson invited her to Galena. When Worthington saw the bare walls of the Yukon Inn, she offered to paint them. Benson was a fan of Robert Service and asked her to illustrate *The Shooting of Dan McGrew*. She wrote the words with brushes and drew the illustrations with Italian chalks directly on the walls, using mostly locals as models. Working also as a bartender and cook, it took her almost three years to finish. Worthington left Galena shortly after and was tragically killed in a plane crash in 1969. No one who saw these illustrations ever forgot them. Fortunately, Ken Lavigne, from New Hampshire, had them photographed in 1974 and reproduced. He then hung the reproductions in his own bar, Ken's Pipeline, in Fairbanks. Lavigne died in 2004 and some of the reproductions were sold at auction.

Joe and Pat Cooper moved to Galena in 1969, where Joe worked as the school principal. On their website, the *Christmas Party at Hobo's* story describes the bar as "the roughest, filthiest, pest hole on the Yukon River," the clientele as "three distinct racial groups," Benson as "a very charitable man," and the midnight raffle where Benson announced that the winning ticket holder—a local soldier—got his pick of three young women to spend the rest of the night with.

1977 was a big year for the Yukon Inn. In March, a fire destroyed the Yukon and the illustrations. In May, Benson sold the Yukon to William Kendall, who re-built it. In July, the bar was full of customers celebrating the Yukon 800 boat race. In August, Kendall was busted for selling bootleg beer from the bar. In 1979, Benson bought the bar back and in 1983 he moved the Yukon Inn to its current location and changed the name to Hobo's Yukon Inn. Benson passed away in 1990.

Archie Thurmond, an Alaska native from Nulato, bought the Yukon Inn in 1991. Thurmond continued the tradition of providing a place where locals and visitors could get a good drink in Galena until his death in 2001. Marlene Marshall, daughter of Thurmond, and her husband Victor bought the bar in 2002. During Memorial Day weekend in 2013, Galena experienced the worst flood in one hundred years, and the bar suffered significant damage. It was closed for months but reopened. Marlene Marshall passed away in 2015.

➤**Visiting the Yukon Inn:** This is the only bar in Galena and the only bar along the Yukon River from Tanana to the Bering Sea (approximately six hundred miles). The Yukon Inn is rustic but has all the amenities anyone could need. It is also the unofficial social center of Galena and is the place to be for all the major holidays.

FRANK "HOBO" BENSON OUTSIDE THE MAIN ENTRANCE OF THE YUKON INN.

Frank Benson (1924 – 1990) at the Yukon Inn.
From The Untold Story of Hobo and Dangerous Dan McGrew *by Ken Lavigne – 1975*

Joe's Bar
34 Tonzona Avenue, McGrath
(907) 524-3466

License Issued: September 29, 1970, to Joseph and Caroline Degnan
Amenities: Pool table, darts, TV, food, occasional live music, liquor store
Find them Online: Facebook

History and Notoriety: Many thanks to the late Sally Jo Collins of the Tochak Historical Society in McGrath who provided much of what follows.

Joe's Bar was first known as the Morris Roadhouse, owned by Lawrence "Jack" Morris. Born in New York state, Morris came to McGrath in 1930. When the Takotna River changed course in 1937, he bought the old Kruhm Roadhouse buildings and moved them to the new McGrath townsite. One building was the bar and dance hall and the other the kitchen and dining area and guest rooms. In 1948, Jack hired his sister Sally to manage the bar. Fire destroyed both buildings in 1951. Morris then bought an old Army mess hall building, moved it to his lot, and converted it into the new roadhouse, with a modern cocktail lounge, restaurant, and lodging. Opening day was April 26, 1952.

Morris sold the roadhouse to his sister Sally in 1956 and moved to the Lower 48. She died in 1957, and Morris came back to manage the bar until it was sold to Barbara Rogers in 1959. In 1965, Rogers sold the bar to R.L. "Pat" and Mary Neeley who changed the name to Pat's Roadhouse. In 1967, Robert Magnuson and Gerald Timmons bought the bar and changed the name to the McGrath Roadhouse. In 1970, Joseph "Joe" and Caroline Degnan became the new owners.

Joe was born in Connecticut in 1912, and Caroline was born in Washington in 1916. They had worked together as miners in the

Ophir area since the late 1930s. They were a congenial couple, and people began referring to the roadhouse as Joe's Bar. Joe Degnan passed away in 1988, and Caroline later that same year. Caroline's grandniece, Valkyrie Magnuson, inherited the bar at the young age of twenty-one. Magnuson officially changed the name to Joe's Bar on August 2, 1990, and the cafe to Caroline's Kitchen. Tragically, Magnuson was killed in a snowmobile accident in 2007. The bar is still owned by the Magnuson family.

☛Visiting Joe's Bar: The exterior has changed but the interior still has some of the original Morris Roadhouse furnishings. Their old website stated that Joe's is the "oldest bar on the river." If you were to count the years that it was the Morris Roadhouse and then the McGrath Roadhouse, it is. When the Iditarod sled dog race comes to town (in March) and Halloween are popular times to be at Joe's.

Joe's Bar in 2008.
Photo courtesy of Steve Kovach

Inside the Beachcombers Bar, Kodiak – circa 1980, 1855 Mission Road 1944-1989. From the Beachcombers *Facebook page*

NOTORIOUS BARS OF SOUTHWEST ALASKA

NOTE: Dillingham bars are listed in the Western Alaska chapter

- **Dillingham**
- **Naknek** (3 bars)
- **King Salmon** (1 bar)
- **Kodiak** (5 bars)

ALASKA PENINSULA

N

Southwest Alaska

B & B Bar
326 Shelikof Street, Kodiak
(907) 486-3575

License issued: September 1944 to Jesse Blinn and George Blinn
Amenities: Pool table
Find them Online: Facebook

History and Notoriety: The first B & B opened in 1899 and was owned by Perley D. "Captain" Blodgett and Jesse M. "Jack" Blinn (Blodgett and Blinn, or booze and beer). The bar was located on Main Street near the Alaska Commercial Company, now the Kodiak History Museum. A photograph from that year shows seven patrons and the bartender inside the bar. The photo has been circulated and reproduced in several Alaskan books, magazines, and newspapers.

Blodgett was born in Vermont in 1855 and Blinn was born in Indiana in 1862. Blodgett was Superintendent of the Cook Inlet Transportation Company from 1903 – 1916, which provided steamship service between Seldovia and other Cook Inlet towns, hence his "Captain" nickname. Blinn managed the Northern Commercial Company (NCC) store on Woody Island in 1888, and then the NCC store in Kodiak.

Their partnership included opening a sawmill and a salmon cannery on Kodiak Island in 1911. Prohibition closed the bar in 1918 which prompted Blinn to turn it into Blinn's Cigar Store and later a pool hall. Blodgett moved to Seattle in 1919 where he passed away two years later. In 1934, Blinn obtained a retail liquor license and opened a liquor store. He passed away in 1942, and his sons Jesse ("Jess") and George took over the pool hall and liquor store. In 1944, the brothers got a license for a cocktail bar and decided to bring back the B & B name. Opening night was October 3, 1944. George Blinn sold his interest in the bar to Jess in 1946.

In 1949, Jess Blinn and his wife Frieda partnered with Stan Nelson to manage to the B & B Bar and Blinn's Liquor Store. Frieda passed away in 1959 and Jess married Anna in 1962. The 1964 earthquake and tsunami inflicted minimal damage to the bar. In 1968, the bar was sold to Jim and Marlyss (daughter of Jess and Frieda Blinn) Eggemeyer. That same year, the building was moved to its current location. The Eggemeyers restored the building, which is one of the oldest in Kodiak. Anna Blinn bought the bar in 1971 and then sold it to Robert Murray in 1974. Tim Abena bought the bar in 1982, and Lanny Monteiro bought it in 1999, and still owns it today.

The B & B takes great pride in its history. The bar has advertised itself as "Alaska's Oldest Licensed Bar in Alaska's Oldest Town" since the 1970s. The bar proudly displays a copy of its 1906 liquor license in a glass case on the wall.

☛**Visiting the B & B**: The bar has always been a no-frills establishment and is a great place to have a no-frills beverage. Note the "Dead Men Tell No Tales" sign on the inside of the front door. The bar has an annual "Bag Ladies Ball" in April which includes a costume contest.

"Captain" Perley D. Blodgett, circa 1900.

Jesse M. "Jack" and Clara Blinn, circa 1900.
Photos courtesy of Beoma Blinn Oakley

Tony's Bar
518 West Marine Way, Kodiak
(907) 486-9489

License issued: 1934 to Anton Kvas
Amenities: Pool tables, dart boards, TVs, occasional live music, liquor store
Find them Online: http://www.tonysbarak.com/; Facebook

History and Notoriety: Anton "Tony" Kvas was born in Yugoslavia in 1888 and was living in Kodiak in 1922. By 1934, Kvas owned his own hotel and bar. In 1940, ads in the *Kodiak Mirror* boasted that Tony's Tavern had "All brands of beer – ice cold," "The largest selection of whiskeys and wines in Kodiak" and "The Best Cuba Libras in Town" (dark rum, Coca Cola, and lime). Later that year, ads claimed that Tony's had "The Longest Bar in Alaska."

Joseph Driscoll, in his book *War Discovers Alaska* described Tony's in the year 1943. "Night life centers on Tony's, where a buxom, pleasant Negro woman from Bakersfield, California, plays the piano and is amazed at the numbers requested by the patrons, selections from Martha and Samson and Dalilah and high-class stuff like that. Tony's one-woman floor show formerly played on cruise ships, but she prefers her present job as a sort of Elsie Janis or Gracie Fields in blackface. She tells me you couldn't wish for more musically inclined patrons than the construction workers and soldiers of Alaska. Moreover, it has been her experience that the tougher a town is, the more polite are the customers toward piano-playing ladies, no matter what color their skin may be."

Kvas married Goldie Jones in 1943, suffered a stroke in 1945, and signed over the bar to Goldie in 1946. He passed away in 1948. In 1952, Harry and Elinor Gottschalk and Lila Bowman bought Tony's. Lila Gottschalk became the sole owner in 1956 and sold the bar to Mildred Markham and Von Straut in 1962. The 1964 earthquake and tsunami lifted Tony's and moved it to Benson Avenue. Tony's was later reconstructed at its current location on the Mall. Markham was the primary owner 1970 – 1989 when Andrew Lundquist took over. George and Patty Gatter bought the building in 2002 and the bar in 2007.

Tony's has used the terms tavern, bar, and place over the years. It has been remodeled many times. Because Tony's is large and open every day of the year, it remains the most popular bar in town. It no longer boasts as having the longest bar in Alaska. Instead, the current motto is "Biggest Navigational Hazard on Kodiak."

> **Visiting Tony's Bar:** Tony's is the place to be during the Kodiak Crab Festival held on the third weekend in May, which includes live music, and an arm-wrestling competition. Halloween and New Year's Eve are very popular times to be at Tony's.

Tony and Goldie Kvas – circa 1943.
Property of Kodiak History Museum (P-418-1-90)

Village Bar
408 East Marine Way, Kodiak
(907) 486-3412

License issued: 1957 to Dorothy M. Cummings and Irene J. Hansen
Amenities: Pool tables, dart boards, TVs, occasional live music
Find them Online: https://village-bar-kodiak.edan.io/

History and Notoriety: The Village Bar has its roots in a bar known as Club Unique, which opened in 1945. In 1957, Dorothy Cummings and Irene Hansen bought the Club Unique and changed the name to the Village Bar. Barbara "Barb" Williams replaced Hansen in 1958 and became sole owner in 1963. She installed a miniature bowling alley and made other improvements that attracted a loyal following.

Williams sold the bar to Virginia Wilson in 1963. The bar sustained significant damage during the 1964 earthquake. Rollyn "Ron" Ball re-opened the bar in its current location on the Mall in 1968. The Ball family still owns the bar.

For several years the bar adjoined a restaurant called the Polar Bear Café, which opened in 1942. Eventually the bar absorbed the restaurant. There was once a piano and a fireplace, which were typical of Alaska bars during the 1960s. The bar served an "Alaska Cocktail" that contained six shots with a splash of juice. Those who finished one kept the signature glass.

☛Visiting the Village Bar: The Village is between the Mecca and Tony's, which makes it very convenient for bar crawls. If you're doing a crawl, stop in and count how many fish are in the fish tank. Monday Night Football is a popular time to be at the Village. The bar is closed for Thanksgiving and Christmas.

*The Polar Bear restaurant and the Village Bar in 1962.
Photo courtesy of Amanda Kiefer*

Mecca Lounge
302 West Marine Way, Kodiak
(907) 486-3364

License issued: 1940 to Roy F. Snyder
Amenities: Darts, TVs, occasional live entertainment
Find them Online: Facebook

History and Notoriety: Roy Snyder was born in Nebraska in 1893. In 1933, he was managing a beer parlor and card room named the Mecca in McCarthy. When the Kennecott Mine closed in 1938, he moved to Kodiak and opened the Mecca Bar. Snyder soon began making plans for a nightclub. The grand opening of the Mecca Cocktail Lounge was on June 23, 1941. According to the

Kodiak Mirror, the lounge boasted sliding doors made of mahogany, Philippine mahogany wainscoting around the lower part of the walls, parchment wall murals in soft pastel colors, a tile dance floor, a piano, a jukebox, and private booths of leather and chromium. Add to that the venetian blinds, curtains, and neon lights, it is no wonder that Snyder boasted that the Mecca was "the most beautiful cocktail lounge in Alaska—bar none, even in Juneau." A tough rule of the house was that men unattended by a lady were not admitted.

In 1945, Snyder bought the Reception bar in Fairbanks, which he re-named the Mecca. In December 1958, on the brink of Alaska statehood, the Mecca in Kodiak added a restaurant, naming it the 49 Room. The name changed to the Mecca Harborview in 1979 and to the Mecca Restaurant in 1982. The Mecca operates today strictly as a bar.

Just like Tony's and the Village, the Mecca moved to the Mall after the 1964 earthquake. A very unfortunate casualty of the earthquake was all of the original furnishings that Snyder invested. Snyder passed away in 1974. The Snyder family owned the Mecca in Kodiak until 1978, when William Bishop took over.

☛**Visiting the Mecca Lounge:** The Mecca is normally open only on Fridays and Saturdays, usually from 10 p.m. to 4 a.m., where primarily a younger crowd congregates after the other bars are winding down.

From Lou Jacobin's Guide to Alaska and the Yukon – 1971.

The Rendezvous
11652 West Rezanof Drive (Chiniak Highway), Kodiak
(907) 487-2233

License issued: 1956 to Theodore and Louise Schwartz
Amenities: Pool table, darts, food, occasional live entertainment
Find them Online: Facebook

History and Notoriety: The Rendezvous Bar was first located at Middle Bay, about seven miles further south from the current location. According to Tony Smaker, who compiled stories about life at the Kodiak Tracking Station during the 1950s and '60s "It was a real 'Alaskan' watering hole complete with deer horns, game skins, and the like on the walls. Also, some other types of controversial stuffed game models like the dreaded three-horned jack-a-squirrel, the very rare-indeed Kodiak trained killer bear (back end of a bear, front end a Marine with MSGT stripes), and of course the usual collection of 'Polish' war equipment like shotguns, saws, and the like." The bar burned down in 1987 and was re-built as a home. James and Betty Fitzjearl bought the license in 1988 and moved the bar to its current location.

Toni Munsey and Val Flinders took over in 2002, and the bar acquired a reputation for booking high quality entertainment. Some of the best musicians in Alaska have played here and the bar has autographed posters to prove it. Some famous Lower 48 folk and blues bands (Cheryl Wheeler, Kelly Joe Phelps, Walter Trout, Kenny Acosta) have been here too. The small size of the bar—seventy people maximum occupancy—guaranteed that the performances were intimate and memorable.

Munsey decorated the bar with a variety of colorful paintings and realistic creations of marine life. The bar has craft cocktails, which aren't always easy to find on the island.

☛**Visiting The Rendezvous:** The bar is just ten minutes from the Kodiak airport. If you're with some friends, consider using the "shotski" (a ski with four shot glasses attached). Note the surfboard with inscriptions to those who have passed on.

The first Rendezvous Bar – circa 1956.
Property of Kodiak History Museum (P-596-1_Rendezvous)

Eddie's Fireplace Inn
(a.k.a. Eddie's; a.k.a. E.F.I.)
1 Main Street, King Salmon
(907) 246-3435

License Issued: November 6, 1975, to Edgar K. Oaks Jr.
Amenities: Darts, TV, food, occasional live music
Find them Online: Facebook

History and Notoriety: This restaurant and bar was first known as the King Salmon Inn. The owners, Arnold "Arnie" and Catherine Omholt had previously managed the Curry Hotel on the Alaska Railroad until it was destroyed by fire in 1957. They moved to King Salmon in 1958, bringing the Curry Hotel liquor license with them. Catherine Omholt died in 1973, and Arnie sold the bar to Edgar "Eddie" Oaks Jr. in 1975.

Oaks, from California, joined the US Army and moved to

Alaska in 1946. He moved to King Salmon in 1958, where he and his wife Lucy managed the King Salmon Commercial Co. Oaks opened the now-closed King-Ko Inn in 1971 and sold it April 1, 1975. He then bought the King Salmon Inn and renamed it Eddie's Fireplace Inn. Oaks loved catering to the locals and tourists alike. It is his smiling face that is shown on the bar sign. He owned the bar until his death in 1999. Michael Swain Sr. bought the bar and is the current owner.

☞Visiting Eddie's Fireplace Inn: Eddie's is within easy walking distance of the King Salmon airport, which makes it popular with travelers who want to eat and have a drink. During the Bristol Bay "Winterfest" in February and "Fishtival" in July, events such as the chili cook-off and poker and cribbage tournaments can be found here.

Fisherman's Bar
Mile 0 Alaska Peninsula Highway, Naknek
(907) 246-4252

License Issued: 1951 to Joseph C. and Josephine S. Huard
Amenities: Pool tables, darts, foosball, TVs, food, occasional live music, liquor store
Find them Online: Facebook

History and Notoriety: This bar opened the same year that motors were first allowed to propel small fishing boats operating on Bristol Bay. True to its name, this bar is still a favorite watering hole of commercial fishermen and cannery workers.

According to Jennie Nelson in her book *Remembering Naknek*, Joseph "Joe" Huard was from Canada, and had been a professional dancer in New York City. He moved to Alaska in 1934, served in the US Army in WWII, married an Alaska Native woman who died giving birth to twin girls, and later married Josephine. Huard loved to party and was famous for telling stories and jumping up on the bar to tap dance. During the 1950s, bars in Naknek would blare music to announce that they were open, and Huard was very fond of this practice.

By 1958, Huard had a business partner named Naomi Douglas. To entertain the customers, Huard would play the banjo, and Douglas would sing and play the piano. The partners married in 1959. In 1973, they sold the bar to Paul Brannon and Gary Bradford. Huard died in 1983, but the adjoining liquor store still uses his name. In 1982, Bradford and his wife Jo Ann became the owners. The couple donated a yearly percentage of the bar profits to the St. Theresa's Catholic Church in Naknek. Jo Ann Bradford passed away in 1998 and the church erected a statue of Saint Theresa as a memorial to her generosity.

Over the years, Fisherman's has been the scene of many barroom brawls. In 1980, local fishermen clashed with fishermen working for Icicle Seafoods, which had just been bought by a Japanese conglomerate. When a strike was organized by the locals to hold out for better prices, the Icicle fishermen ignored it and went fishing. Ugly, vicious fights broke out at the Fisherman's Bar, as well as Hadfield's and other Bristol Bay bars.

In 2020, a man stole a fire truck from the King Salmon Fire Station and drove fifteen miles with lights flashing to the Fisherman's Bar, where he was arrested.

> **Visiting the Fisherman's Bar:** The locals know that this is the place to come for karaoke. When I visited, I was impressed when the bartender, an attractive brunette, grabbed the mike and not only sang but walked around the entire bar. The bar sponsors a pool tournament here during the Bristol Bay Winterfest in February and Fishtival in July.

From the Bristol Bay News – *May 1, 1959.*

Hadfield's Bar
Mile .1 Alaska Peninsula Highway, Naknek
(907) 246-4441

License Issued: 1953 to Robert K. and Erma B. Hadfield
Amenities: Pool table, darts, foosball, TVs, food, occasional live music, liquor store
Find them Online: Facebook

History and Notoriety: This bar was once known as Herman's Place, owned by Herman Sandvik and Robert "Bob" Hadfield in 1947. Hadfield was born in 1913 in Seattle and worked as a commercial fisherman. He visited his brother Jack in Anchorage and met Erma Bernadine "Bernie" the sister of Jack's wife Helen. Bernie was also from Washington state, and she and Hadfield married in 1940. They were living in Naknek in 1947 but moved to Washington, returning in 1953. They took over the business, which had been renamed the Naknek Hotel and Bar, and now included a restaurant and liquor store. The Hadfields began making improvements to the bar. Ads in the *Bristol Bay News* from the early 1960s touted that the bar featured pool tables, bowling, a shuffleboard, and a dance floor.

In 1959, an anchor from an old wooden ship was discovered in the Naknek harbor and brought to Hadfield's. The anchor was later identified as being from the *Charles E. Moody*, which was destroyed by fire in the harbor in 1920. The vessel had once brought fishermen and supplies to Naknek. The anchor still reposes in front of the bar.

In 1979, the Naknek Hotel (now the D & D Hotel) and the bar became two separate businesses. The Hadfields continued to operate the bar and officially changed the name to Hadfield's Bar. Bob Hadfield passed away in 1983, and Bernie and their son Robert G. managed the bar until Bernie passed in 1989. Robert Hadfield and Trish Brackebush are the current owners.

> **☛Visiting Hadfield's Bar:** This is a good place to hear local musicians. The Halloween party with costume contest is popular here. During the Bristol Bay Winterfest in February, the bar holds turkey bowling and spam cookoff competitions.

From the Bristol Bay News *– June 1971.*

Bristol Bay Red Dog Inn
2 Monsen Street, Naknek
(907) 246-4215

License Issued: 1973 to Alphus and Winifred Alford
Amenities: Pool table, darts, TV, food, occasional live music
Find them Online: Facebook

History and Notoriety: This bar was first known as Patsy's, owned by James "Jimmie" Pierce and his wife Patricia "Patsy" in the 1940s. In the book *Alaska's Lost Frontier,* author Denton Moore wrote that Patsy used to work as a prostitute in Nome. She boasted that she knew most of the early Alaskan upper crust—judges, lawyers, businessmen—but that she only recognized them when they had their pants off. She continued to run the bar and serve meals after Jimmie Pierce died. Patsy Pierce was a very generous person who was loved by all; all of Naknek would celebrate her birthday.

In 1956, Patsy Pierce passed away and Jennie Nelson bought the bar, changing the name to Jennie's. Nelson had moved to Naknek in 1952 from Washington state, had worked at the Naknek Hotel, and owned the local Anchor Bar. Nelson loved to serve gourmet meals and exotic drinks. In a town like Naknek, where the clientele often wore hip boots and smelled like fish, this was a much-needed touch of class. The bar was decorated with paintings, glass balls, fish nets, floats, skis and snowshoes, and an organ from a church in the ghost town of Kanatak. When Nelson left Alaska in 1972, her antiques were donated to the Bristol Bay Museum in Naknek. She later wrote a book about her experiences, titled *Remembering Naknek*. Nelson passed away in 1999.

Alphus and Winifred "Winnie" Alford bought the bar in 1973, changing the name to the Red Dog Inn. The couple was already well-known in town and had always supported the local fishermen. A 1980 article in the *Bristol Bay News* titled "El Rojo Pero Cantina" stated that the bar "...has been involved directly with the establishment of local control of fish production and marketing since the official start in 1975." The article also referred to the bar as an "institution" to the locals and as a "happening" to the transients and tourists. Alphus Alford passed away in 2018, and Winnie sold the bar to Melissa Davis in 2022.

>**Visiting the Bristol Bay Red Dog Inn:** While sharing a similar name with the famous bar in Juneau, the bar is different and unique. The bumper sticker collection dates to the 1970s. Saturday and Sunday brunch is always good here.

Sand Point Tavern
(a.k.a. Shumagin Tavern)
Lot 16, Sand Point
(907) 383-5050

License Issued: 1960 to Robert N. Williamson
Amenities: Pool tables, darts, foosball, TV, food, occasional live music
Find them Online: http://www.shumagin.com/business-opportunities/sand-point-tavern/

History and Notoriety: Sand Point has an interesting history of gold mining, fish processing and canning. Robert Williamson took on Jack Foster as a partner in 1967, and the tavern moved to its current location in 1973. Foster and his wife Mae took control of the tavern in 1975 and sold it to Richard and Ruth Farrens in 1980. In 1985 the bar was sold to the Shumagin Corporation, the Alaska Native village corporation for Sand Point created under the 1971 Alaska Native Claims Settlement Act.

In 1993, Sand Point police responded to a call from the manager of the Sand Point Tavern concerning an intoxicated person. Two officers were escorting the patron out of the tavern when they were accosted by other patrons, resulting in a brawl. The police chief arrived at the tavern and assisted his officers in arresting a number of the patrons. Following this incident, a group of citizens circulated a petition calling for the dismissal of the police chief. It was signed by at least 120 residents and stated that the chief should be removed from office due to the use of excessive force in making arrests at the Sand Point Tavern. The petition also stated that the chief had "created a situation where people will not call the police for help because they are afraid of the police." The police chief was removed from office.

☛Visiting the Sand Point Tavern: There is no sign announcing you've arrived at the Tavern. Karaoke is popular here, and there is lots of room for dancing, but the clientele usually opts for the usual bar games.

Last Hook Off
136 Park Avenue, King Cove
(907) 497-2312

License Issued: August 1, 1983, to King Cove Corporation (Rudolph Mack, President)
Amenities: Pool tables, TV, food, occasional live music
Find them Online: Facebook (King Cove Corporation)

History and Notoriety: Founded in 1911, the primary industry in King Cove is fishing, and the boats work both sides of the Alaska Peninsula searching for salmon. At the end of the season, however, the fish come to King Cove. The final seining set of the season, known as the "hook off," is sometimes right off the King Cove beach.

The Last Hook Off is run by the King Cove Corporation, the local Alaska Native corporation formed under the Alaska Native Claims Settlement Act of 1971. When it first opened, there was a local controversy over Alaska Natives owning a bar. The bar is in the same building as the hotel and corporation office, and its windows look out at the cove. The horseshoe shaped bar runs ninety-seven feet, which was touted as the longest in Alaska when it first opened.

King Cove has been in the news since the early 1990s because of the desire of the city to have a one-lane gravel road built through the Izembek National Wildlife Refuge and wilderness area to the town of Cold Bay so that sick or injured residents could have access to an all-weather airport. The US Department of the Interior selected the "no action" alternative to the Environmental Impact Statement, primarily because the refuge shelters millions of migratory waterfowl. Environmental groups oppose a road through the refuge and wilderness for the precedent it would set. Another reason I've heard is that the road would be a big (and potentially dangerous) temptation for patrons drinking at the Last Hook Off, or at the bar in Cold Bay, to check out the action at the other end of the road.

☛**Visiting the Last Hook Off:** The bar is large, with a big dance floor and lots of booths. King Cove has a small population, but on some nights during fishing season, it can be hard to find a spot at the bar.

Akutan Roadhouse
(a.k.a. Road House Tavern)
Foot Trail, Akutan
(907) 698-2219

License Issued: 1972 to Robert Pelkey Sr.
Amenities: Pool table, darts, TV, food, occasional live music
Find them Online: Facebook

History and Notoriety: Robert "Bob" Pelkey, from Washington state, came to Akutan in 1959. In his memoir titled *Off the Map: The True Adventures of Robert L. Pelkey, Sr.* he describes how the villagers would brew their own booze using raisins, which they called "Raisin Jack." Pelkey thought the village needed an alternative to the grog, and in 1966, he built a tavern. He served only beer (a tradition that continues to this day) believing that hard alcohol has a negative effect on small villages like Akutan. Pelkey sold the bar in 1968 and moved his family back to Washington. Three years later, he returned to Akutan and bought the bar back but had to rebuild it. He named the new bar the Akutan Roadhouse because of his love of driving.

In the book, Pelkey writes about the Norwegian and Icelandic fishermen that would frequent the bar and start arm wrestling after a few beers. This sometimes led to full-fledge brawls, which always resulted in broken furniture. He also described the 1989 murder of his brother-in-law, who was having a very successful night at the pool table and was stabbed by a man he had beaten. One man was charged with murder and another man with assault.

Pelkey died in 2003 at age 63 in an ultralight airplane crash near Anchorage. Fortunately, he had tape recorded his adventures, which were made into his memoir. Anita Pelkey, his widow, and the Pelkey family still own the bar.

In 2007, Captain Sig Hansen and his *Northwestern* crew of crab fishermen from the *Deadliest Catch* TV series visited the Akutan Roadhouse. Their visit was included in the episode being filmed. Some of the fishermen of the *Time Bandit* (another *Deadliest Catch* crew) have also visited the bar.

> **Visiting the Akutan Roadhouse**: The exterior disguises the relaxed atmosphere inside. Check out the wall of framed photos of fishing vessels and the wooden table engraved with signatures. While you can get a glass for your beer, the beer is still served in a can.

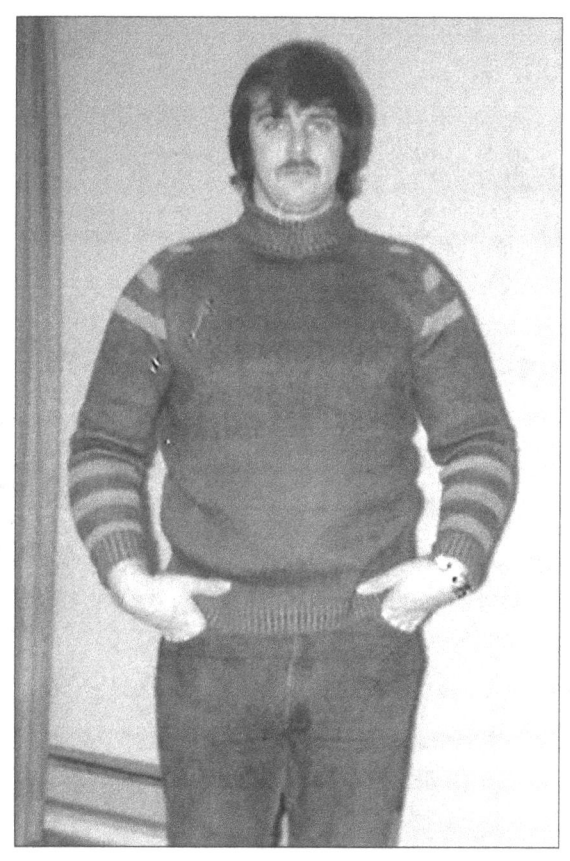

Bob Pelkey in 1973.
From the Akutan Roadhouse *Facebook page*

*Bering Sea Saloon, Nome – 2007.
313 Front Street 1946 – 2012.*

NOTORIOUS BARS OF WESTERN ALASKA

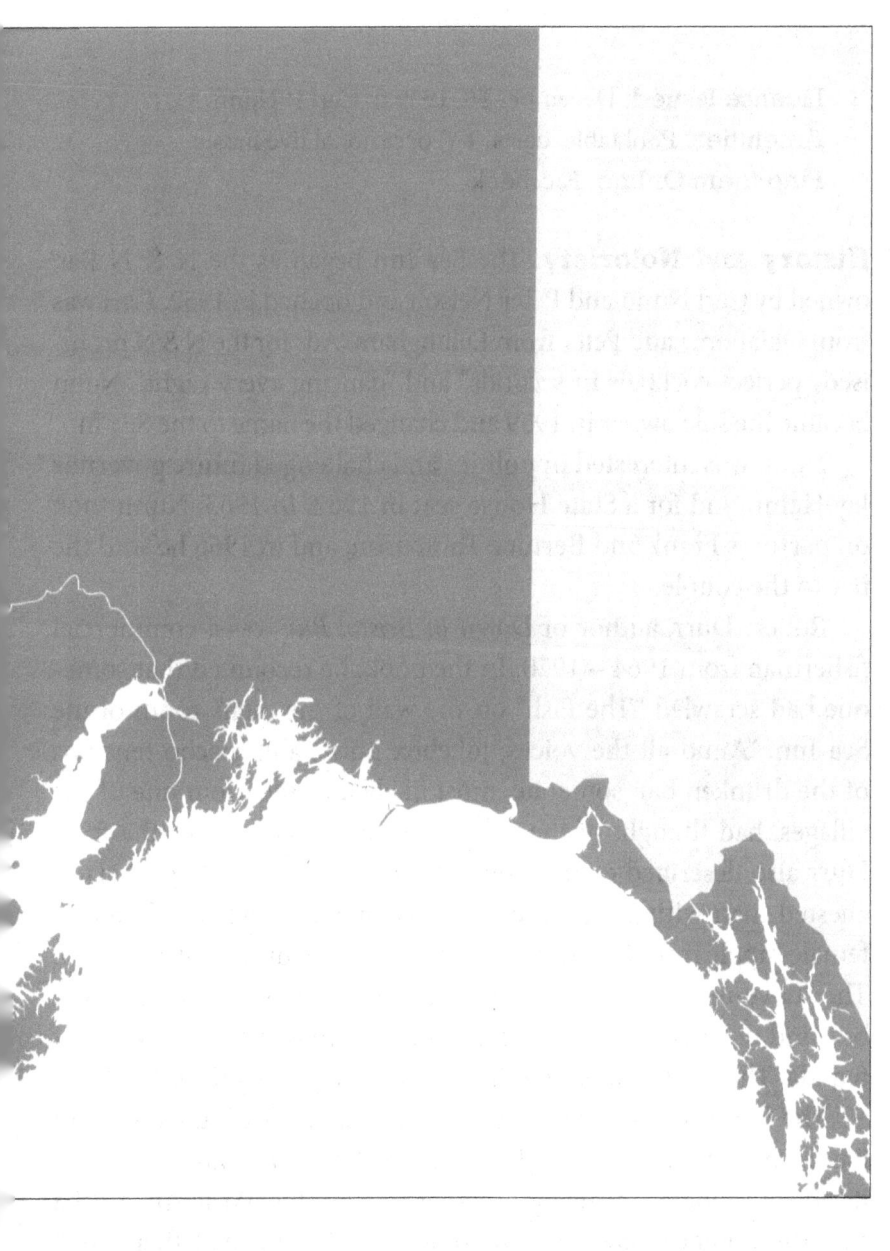

Sea Inn
8 Alley Way, Dillingham
(907) 842-2233

License Issued: December 30, 1959 to Carl P. Nunn
Amenities: Pool table, darts, TV, occasional live music
Find them Online: Facebook

History and Notoriety: The Sea Inn began as the N & N Bar, owned by Carl Nunn and Peter Nelson and opened in 1952. Carl was from Oklahoma and Peter from Dillingham. Ads for the N &N promised "perfect cocktails in seconds" and "dancing every night." Nunn became the sole owner in 1959 and changed the name to the Sea Inn.

Nunn was interested in politics and challenged future governor Jay Hammond for a State House seat in 1962. In 1963, Nunn took on partners Frank and Bernice Thomason, and in 1966 he sold the bar to the couple.

Robert Durr, author of *Down in Bristol Bay* was a commercial fisherman from 1964 – 1970. In the book, he recounted that someone had scrawled "The Fish" on the wall of the men's room of the Sea Inn. "Amid all the voices, jukebox noise, and macho tensions of the drunken bar, someone, most likely a Native from one of the villages, had thought of the fish, the rudimentary fact of the fish." Durr also described owner Frank Thomason ("a very large, barrel-chested man with a big nose and permanently fierce eyes") and a female hippie from California who was dancing by herself at the bar. The "Love-in Girl" was wearing a miniskirt, a loose shirt without a bra, and no shoes. The event prompted Thomason to pour shots of tequila. The Thomasons sold the bar to Shirley Wiggins in 1982.

The Sea Inn can be a rowdy place during the fishing season and has earned the motto "Sea Inn until you can't see out." However, it accommodates other groups as well. The Western Alaska Interdisciplinary Science Conference and Forum had their 2012 Kick-Off social here.

☛Visiting the Sea Inn: Karaoke is popular here, as the singing walrus on the bar sign indicates. The Beaver Roundup in early March and Independence Day are popular times to be at the Sea Inn.

Willow Tree
513 Wood River Road, Dillingham
(907) 842-2220

License Issued: 1941 to John L. Pearson
Amenities: Pool tables, darts, TV, occasional live music
Find them Online: Facebook (The Willow Tree Bar)

History and Notoriety: John Pearson, born in Sweden in 1902, and his wife Leta, from Michigan, opened Pearson's Tavern and the adjacent Willow Tree Inn in 1941. The location of the Willow Tree was then, as it is today, just outside of town. The Tavern was where the bar, card and pool tables were found. Dancing, food, and pinochle games were at the Willow Tree, including live music every Wednesday and Saturday nights during summer and a special ball every New Years Eve.

From 1936 to 1959, the bars in the Bristol Bay area were prohibited from selling liquor during the two-month fishing season. John Pearson was adept at gathering enough signatures to petition the Clerk of the Court in Juneau for an exception to the law for his tavern. In 1950, he didn't get enough signatures, which prompted him to write an editorial in *The Beacon* (the local newspaper) that accused the conservative folks in town of sabotage.

In 1961, the Pearsons combined both businesses into the Willow Tree Inn and Tavern. In 1963, they sold the bar to Paul G. "P.G." and Emily "Dolly" Brannon who moved the bar to a new location. The bar moved to its current location in 1970.

Robert Durr, author of *Down in Bristol Bay*, was a commercial fisherman from 1964 – 1970. In addition to visiting the Sea Inn, he also frequented the Willow Tree. He described P.G. Brennan, who was also a cannery boss, as "a tall, slow-talking southern transplant with charisma. He kept a jug in his desk drawer, knowing his fishermen, and plied it as occasion warranted." He described the Willow Tree as "an oasis of ease amid the surrounding desert of stress." In 1979, the Brannons' sold the bar to Carl Heyano.

In 1983, Beat Generation poet and environmental activist Gary Snyder wrote *Dillingham, Alaska, the Willow Tree Bar*. The poem describes oil drill workers meeting at a bar after work. He describes them as *"Drinking it down, the pain, of the work, of wrecking the world."* One interpretation of the poem is that the men are drinking to forget that their jobs are destroying the natural environment.

In 1986, owner Heyano was inside the Willow Tree when it burned down due to a fire of "suspicious origin." He suffered minor burns and smoke inhalation.

In 1987, the Brannon's son Rance "Hutchie" Brannon bought the newly rebuilt bar. In a 1991 article in the *Anchorage Daily News*, he described misconceptions about the liquor industry, such as people blaming the business for drunks. He also stated that police would hassle him about his bar, claiming that the Willow Tree was too noisy. After eleven disorderly conduct citations, he showed that the Dillingham city hall produced a higher decibel level (fifty-seven) than his bar (fifty-six). Tragically, Hutchie died in 2004 at the young age of fifty in a motorcycle accident in Anchorage.

In 2012, the Willow Tree made national news when it obtained a one-day exception from the Dillingham law prohibiting the sale of alcohol on a Sunday, specifically Super Bowl Sunday. Then owner Kim Parker served forty pounds of shrimp and flew in seven kegs of beer from an Anchorage microbrewery for the occasion.

☛ **Visiting the Willow Tree:** Weekends are very popular at the bar, but trivia night is also a crowd gatherer. Beaver

Roundup in March, the Tony's Run benefit marathon in September, and when Dillingham High School sporting events occur are popular times to be at the Willow Tree.

Ad from The Beacon, September 28, 1950.
The sketch is of the Inn at the first location.

Breakers Bar
243 Front Street, Nome
(907) 443-2531

License Issued: 1948 to Ruth Spicer Gottschalk
Amenities: Pool tables, darts, TV, occasional live music
Find them Online: Facebook

History and Notoriety: Ruth Spicer, from Idaho, moved to Alaska in 1938. In 1948, she and her husband Harry Gottschalk moved to Nome, bought a building on Front Street that had been a shoe store, and opened the Breakers Bar. Bob Renshaw was the third partner in the venture.

In her autobiography titled *Tales and Trails of a Pioneer*, Ruth wrote that her favorite poem was *The Shooting of Dan McGrew* by Robert Service. She hired a young Fairbanks artist named Gordon Nelson to paint two scenes from the poem. Ruth flew to Fairbanks and transported the paintings to the Breakers. The beautiful paintings are still on the same wall and are in remarkable shape for being over seventy years old.

Famous visitors to the Breakers include WWII greats General Jimmy Dolittle (commander of the Doolittle Raid) and General Simon Buckner (Battle of Okinawa). Ruth met her future husband, Fred Brechan, at the Bering Sea Club. Fred and Ruth Brechan left Nome in 1955 and moved to Kodiak, where they opened a second Breakers Bar, which closed in 2003. During that time, Bob Renshaw ran the bar in Nome, adding a false front to the building in 1957. Ruth remained part-owner of the bar until 1974, when Thomas Reardon took control. The colorful Ruth Spicer Brechan passed away in 2011.

By 2000, Reardon had sold the Breakers to Wayne "Herbie" Locke, who dropped dead in the bar in 2004. Locke's brother Ron then took over the bar.

The Breakers has a window and a deck that faces the Bering Sea. The bar has weathered its share of storms. The storm of 1974 sent a thirty-foot wave into the bar which pushed all the customers out onto the street! Devoted friends helped the bar survive the storms of 2004 and 2011 by keeping water pumps going and moving the inventory, including the paintings.

In 2015, during the post-Iditarod arm-wrestling contest at the Breakers, a veteran woman musher named Aliy Zirkle accidently broke the arm of the woman she was arm-wrestling. This incredibly ironic act occurred just ten seconds into the match, and the "sickening pop" was heard by some observers. Zirkle, who was in extremely good shape, said later it was her "First arm wrestling competition and last arm-wrestling competition."

During the 1970s, the motto of the Breakers was "Still a nice place to drink." The current slogan is "We are the party!"

☛Visiting the Breakers Bar: The Breakers is a must-see when you're in Nome—for the Dan McGrew paintings as well as the good cheer. The Iditarod celebrations include a Kick-Off Party, the arm-wrestling contest (!), Hula Girls Night, and Husky Hoe-Down. Corned beef and cabbage are served all day on St. Patrick's Day.

Ruth Spicer Brechan working the scales at the Breakers Bar. Note the paintings in the background. From the article "Nome, Alaska" by Sally Carrighar. Saturday Evening Post, *January 27, 1951. Image courtesy of Cussy Kauer*

Board of Trade Saloon
(a.k.a. B.O.T.)
211 Front Street, Nome
(907) 443-2611

License Issued: July 1, 1933, to Harry R. Phillips and James E. Hewitt
Amenities: Pool tables, darts, TVs, occasional live music
Find them Online: https://www.visitnomealaska.com/businesses/board-of-trade; Facebook

History and Notoriety: The Board of Trade Saloon can rightfully call itself the "Oldest Bar in Nome" as it has been in business continuously since the city was founded in 1900. The "B.O.T." and the Nevada were among the first bars in Nome to begin serving beer after prohibition ended. It has always been located on Front Street but has moved several times. It has been destroyed by fire five times: 1905, 1925, 1926, 1934, and 1950. It has also endured significant storm damage six times: 1902, 1913, 1937, 1942, 1945, and 1946.

Two of the earliest owners of the B.O.T. in Nome (there was another Board of Trade saloon in Skagway) were J.C. Muther and E.V. Adams. During prohibition, the B.O.T. served soft drinks and operated as a card and pool room. Harry Phillips, from England, and his partner James Hewitt, from Ireland, bought the B.O.T. in 1924, and obtained a dispensary license in 1933. By 1944, Arvo "Arv" Saario and Joe Baldridge were the owners. It was Sarrio who coined the B.O.T. slogan "Good Things For He That Is Dry!"

In 1955, Sarrio and his wife Marjorie owned the B.O.T. They sold the bar in 1956 to Thomas and Barbara Martin, who then sold it to Charles "Chuck" Reader and James D. "Jim" West in 1960. By 1964, West and his wife Margaret were the sole owners. Jim was from Arkansas and moved to Alaska in 1951. He was a very successful businessman in Nome and expanded the B.O.T. by taking over the businesses on both sides. He would admit to owning half the town and said that he might buy the rest someday. He would also impress tourists by pulling a wad of thousand-dollar bills wrapped in a rubber band out of his packet. However, he reportedly hated to raise drink prices. The colorful Jim West passed away in 2009 at the age of eighty-two after almost fifty years of managing the B.O.T. His son James West, Jr. is the current owner.

The Board of Trade is one of the most famous and notorious bars in Alaska. It is the largest bar in Nome (seats 125) and is a favorite of Alaska Natives, who come from the surrounding dry villages to drink in Nome. It is also the unofficial headquarters for the celebration of the end of the Iditarod sled-dog race in March. Nomeites and visitors doing a bar tour of Nome, known as the "Nome Shuffle," always end their evening at the B.O.T. (which also stands for "black-out time.")

☛Visiting the Board of Trade Saloon: The Board of Trade takes pride in its history, a tradition that began with Jim West, Sr., and the walls are adorned with photos of Nome, West, the bar, and its customers. Famous visitors include actors Richard Gere, Steven Seagal, Hugh O'Brian, and football great Lyn Swann. The end of the Iditarod, Halloween, and New Year's Eve are wild and crazy times to be at the B.O.T.

Arvo Saario behind the bar at the BOT.
From Alaska Almanac *by William Tewkesbury – 1950*

Polar Bar (Nome)
224 Front Street, Nome
(907) 443-2302

License Issued: May 1, 1939 to George P. Madsen and Keith E. Hedreen
Amenities: Pool tables, darts, TVs, liquor store
Find them Online: https://www.visitnomealaska.com/businesses/polar-bar

History and Notoriety: George Madsen and his wife Margaret, from Seattle, came to Nome in 1936 where George worked at the Nevada Grill. Keith Hedreen and his wife Dorothy Mae, also from Seattle, operated the Polar Taxi in town. George and Keith joined forces and opened the Polar Bar and Grill on May 6, 1939, in the former Cavey's Bakery and Restaurant. The Polar Bar and Grill soon added a hotel and bowling alley.

In 1941, Lieutenant John W. Baum arrived in Nome to determine where to build a US Army garrison, and he and his wife stayed at the Polar Bar hotel. Baum recalled that the bowling alley was open all night, and that the owner's bedroom was located directly above the "impact zone." He also told how his wife was in the Polar Bar one day when she was approached by a "courtly, very courteous, elderly drunk" man who offered her a gold nugget. He emptied the contents of his poke on the table and told her to pick one. She reluctantly took a nugget. When she saw him on the street the next day, she thanked him again, but the old man didn't recognize her.

The bar was popular with the soldiers stationed in Nome, who could get a steak dinner for $2.50. In 1943 Madsen and Hedreen added a liquor store and curio shop. The building suffered significant damage from the October 1945 storm. Both partners were interested in politics, and Madsen served as a Representative to the State House from 1948 – 1952. In 1954 Madsen sold his interest in the business to the Hedreens. That same year, Keith Hedreen was elected a Nome City Councilman. He died in 1969, but Dorothy Mae remained owner until 1974, when she sold the Polar to Ernie and Betty Gustafson. Soon after, a bartender at the Polar invented the "Bering Ball Cocktail." The Krier family are the current owners.

➤**Visiting the Polar Bar:** This bar is popular with folks who like to buy pull-tabs. Note the old photos on the wall that were hung by Betty Gustafson. During the Iditarod, the Polar hosts the popular "Make Your Own Bikini" contest. Contestants must use materials other than fabric to fashion their bikini, leading to hilarious results.

MANY residents believe that when the wind is roaring outside, the Polar Bar is Nome's most comfortable haven.

George Madsen pouring drinks at the Polar Bar.
From Tewkesbury's Alaska Business Directory *– 1948*

Safety Roadhouse
Mile 22 Nome-Council Road, Nome
(907) 443-2368

License Issued: June 14, 1978, to Donald J. Reader
Amenities: Pool table, darts, food, liquor store
Find them Online: Facebook

History and Notoriety: The first radio telegraph station near Nome was constructed at Safety in 1901. By 1910, it was operating as a roadhouse. It burned down in 1919 and was rebuilt. Charles Dalquist, from Minnesota, owned and operated the roadhouse from 1910 until his death in 1950.

The 1925 serum run to Nome made celebrities out of dog musher Gunnar Kaasen and his lead dog Balto, for it was they who carried the antidote for diphtheria the final stretch into the isolated city. However, the plan was for Kaasen to hand over the serum to Ed Rohn at the Safety Roadhouse, where Rohn was waiting with a fresh dog team. The accusation is that Kaasen—or Balto—passed by the roadhouse because he wanted the glory of delivering the serum.

Donald "Johnny" Reader, from North Dakota, managed the Breakers Bar in Nome and bought the roadhouse in 1957. In 1966, it burned down and was rebuilt. Johnny got a liquor license in 1978 but died in 1981. His brother Charles "Chuck" became owner, but the roadhouse burned down again in 1983. Chuck bought the old Nevada Bar building in Nome, cut it into four pieces, and moved it to Safety, where it became the new roadhouse bar. The Reader family still owns the roadhouse.

The Safety Roadhouse is the last checkpoint on the Iditarod Trail before a musher competing in the race makes the final push into Nome. Most mushers sign in, pick up their official bibs, and go. In 1987, champion musher Rick Swenson was only eighteen minutes behind leader Susan Butcher but could not coax his dogs into leaving the Safety Roadhouse. Swenson had run his team too hard and too long to catch Butcher and the dogs simply had to rest. Swenson went inside, had a shot of whiskey, and ended up waiting three hours before his team was ready to push on. By that time, Butcher had won her second Iditarod.

Every year people snowmobile out from Nome to the Safety Roadhouse to see the racers come through and then speed back to town to catch the race finish.

☛**Visiting the Safety Roadhouse**: The bar is a small museum of the Iditarod sled dog race with photos of the mushers, maps of the trail, and many signed dollar bills. The bar is open in March so that it can serve as a checkpoint, and then again from May 1 to October 1. The Safety Roadhouse is a cash only bar.

Community Tavern
(a.k.a. the Tavern; a.k.a. Tribal Lounge; a.k.a. Star Wars)
2050 Venia Minor Street, St. Paul Island
(907) 546-3200

License Issued: October 13, 1977, to Aleut Community of St. Paul Island (Terenty Philemonof Jr., President)
Amenities: Pool table, darts, TVs, food, occasional live music
Find them Online: Facebook (Aleut Community of St. Paul Island)

History and Notoriety: This is the first and only bar without a restaurant that has ever operated in the Pribilof Islands. The tavern has always been owned by the Aleut Community of St. Paul Island. The Philemonof family served as the first managers of the tavern when it was located at 134 Tolstoi Boulevard. The family is well known: Terenty Philemonof Sr. opened the Community Store in 1948, and his son Anthony served as President of the Tanadgusix Corp. for twenty-four years. (the local Alaska Native village corporation formed under ANCSA).

Other families have taken turns managing the tavern. In the 1980s, it was the Melovidov, Lestenkof, and Lekanof families. In the 1990s, it was the Kudrin, Zacharof, and Melovidov (again) families. Melovidov (also spelled Milovidov) is another well-known family. Alexander Milovidov was Manager of the Russian-American Company 1860 – 1867, and Chief of St. Paul Island from 1867 until his death in 1870.

The first time I heard that there was a bar on St. Paul Island, the people telling me about it called the bar "Star Wars." This was because the bar, and the patrons inside, reminded them of the cantina scene in the *Star Wars: A New Hope* (1977) movie. (I have also heard people refer to the old Unisea Bar in Dutch Harbor as the

"Star Wars bar.") No one I've ever talked to who has been to the Community Tavern refers to it as the Community Tavern. Photos of the original tavern from the ABC file show a weather-beaten two-story building. On the inside were orange-colored booths and tables, a noticeable lack of decorations on the white walls, and an antique-looking juke box. The bar served only beer, a practice that continues today.

In 2004, the bar moved to its current location inside a modern concrete building. While some may miss the quirky character of the original tavern, the opinion of most is that the move was a positive one.

☛ **Visiting the Community Tavern:** This remote tavern is frequented by commercial fishermen and workers from the seafood processing plant. A city ordinance prohibits the bar from operating on weekends.

ACKNOWLEDGEMENTS

I RESPECT PEOPLE WHO OWN and operate a bar, especially in Alaska. And I am appreciative of those people who own an historic bar and realize the uniqueness of their establishment. These people understand the importance of my project and are willing to help me in any way they can, usually by contributing photos and/or information, and reviewing my draft write-ups.

Since I haven't lived in Alaska since 2000, and can't always visit when I want to, I have had to correspond remotely with bar owners and friends who still live there.

In putting the third edition of this book together, I received assistance from the following:

In Southeast Alaska, Marjorie Jackson, owner of the Hole in the Wall in Ketchikan; and Christy Tengs Fowler, owner of the Pioneer Bar in Haines. My old buddy Joel Nudelman of Juneau talked with Gail Niemi, owner of the Sandbar. Joel also visited Squirez and put me in touch with the owner Shayla Weeks-Kaiser.

In Southcentral Alaska, Darolyn Ruskin, owner of Eddie's Sports Bar in Anchorage, and former owner Patsy James; Sheilah Buffington, owner of JJ's Lounge in Anchorage, and former owners Jim and Elaine Link, and Diana Kinnebrew; Darwin Biwer, owner of Darwin's Theory in Anchorage; Jean Reilly Boque, owner of Reilly's in Anchorage; Wanda Gates, owner of the Birchwood Saloon in Chugiak; Cheryl Lewis, owner of the Alaskan Hotel Bar in Cordova; Steve White (former owner) and Linda Stillwell (current owner) of the Pioneer Lodge in Willow..

My old buddy Eric Havelock of Sterling reported back from Alice's Champagne Palace in Homer and Kenai Joe's in Kenai; Ben Havelock, son of Eric and my honorary "nephew," visited 4 Royle Parkers in Soldotna and met with owner Eddie Lee. Ben also visited The Place in Kenai and met with owner Grant Gratrix, and the Birchwood Saloon in Chugiak, where he talked with manager Jo Rainwater. Special thanks to Maria Lewis from the Alaska State Historic Preservation Office who told me about the Tee Pee Bar at the Talkeetna Inn.

In Southwest Alaska, I had the privilege of working with Lynn Walker, Curator of the Kodiak History Museum on a temporary exhibit titled "Kodiak's Historic Bars." To work with me on this project, I recruited my friends Toby Sullivan, long-time resident of Kodiak, and Jim Ramaglia from Anacortes, Washington, who grew up in Kodiak. The combined effort of these "history geeks" helped to answer many questions that I've had about the bars of Kodiak and revealed several historic photos that I was unaware. Many thanks to Hannah Wolfe-MacPike, Collections Manager of the Kodiak History Museum for going through boxes of photos with me. Also in Kodiak, I met with Toni Munsey, former owner of the Rendezvous.

Special thanks to Beoma Blinn Oakley, daughter of Jess Blinn of the B & B Bar in Kodiak, who loaned me many historic photos and documents passed down through her family.

In Interior Alaska, I corresponded with Donna Mather, owner of Monroe's Monderosa in Nenana. My long-time friend Debby McAtee of Fairbanks visited the Drop In (which has closed) and sent me lots of photos as well as her impressions.

My wife JoAnn still doesn't share my interest and enthusiasm for the notorious bars of Alaska. However, she is very willing to venture back to the state where she grew up, and patiently wait, while I visit (or revisit) another library, museum, or bar. Much love and many thanks to you CB.

DOUG VANDEGRAFT was born in southern California and received his first degree from Northern Arizona University in 1982. He lived in Alaska from 1983 – 2000. While working as a Cartographer for the Federal Government, he earned a second degree from the University of Alaska Anchorage in 1998. In 2000, he moved to the Washington D.C. area where he served as the first Chief Cartographer for the US Fish and Wildlife Service. In 2016, he became the first Chief of the Geospatial Services Division for the Bureau of Ocean Energy Management. He began his Notorious Bars of Alaska project in 2000, utilizing records housed at the nearby National Archives and books at the Library of Congress. During his fourteen years of research, he made several trips back to Alaska, visiting libraries, historical societies, and bars that he hadn't visited yet. The first edition of *Notorious Bars of Alaska* was published in 2014, and the second edition in 2017. Doug retired from the Federal Government in 2018 and lives with his wife JoAnn in La Conner, WA.

Index of the Notorious Bars

4 Royle Parkers, 106
49'er Bar, 10

A
AJ's Oldtown Steakhouse and Tavern, 123
Akutan Roadhouse, 221
Al's Alaskan Inn, 89
Alaskan Hotel Bar (Cordova), 140
Alaskan Hotel Bar (Juneau), 36
Alice's Champagne Palace, 121
Alpine Inn, 137
Anchor Inn, 97
Arctic Bar, 4
Avenue, The, 66

B
B & B Bar, 202
Badger Den, 182
Barry's Baranof Lounge, 73
Bernie's Bungalow Lounge, 64
Birchwood Saloon, 131
Board of Trade Saloon, 234
Boatel, The, 170
Boon Dox Bar, 183
Bow, The, 108
Breakers Bar, 231
Bristol Bay Red Dog Inn, 217
Brown Bear Saloon, 95
Bubble Room Lounge, 43
Buckaroo Club, 80

C
Cabin Tavern, The, 93
Carousel Lounge, 82
Chatanika Lodge, 189
Chicken Creek Saloon, 187
Clear Sky Lodge, 180
Community Tavern, 240
Craig Inn, 14

Crossroads Lounge, 74

D
Darwin's Theory, 62
Decanter Inn, 117
Down East Saloon, 125

E
Eddie's Fireplace Inn, 212
Eddie's Sports Bar, 87
Ernie's Bar, 26

F
Fairview Inn, 151
Fisherman's Bar, 213
Fishhook Bar, 136
Flamingo Lounge, 101
Flight Deck Bar, 85
Fogcutter Bar, 50
Forelands Bar, 114

G
Gaslight Lounge, 61
Glacier Inn, 16
Glass Door Bar, 54
Golden Eagle Saloon, 173
Great Alaskan Bush Company, 86

H
Hadfield's Bar, 215
Harbor Bar (Haines), 48
Harbor Bar (Petersburg), 22
Hill Bar, 13
Hole in the Wall, 11

Howling Dog Saloon, 188
Hunger Hut Bar, 115

I
Imperial Bar, 41
International Bar, 164

J
JJ's Lounge, 91
Joe's Bar, 196

K
Kenai Joe's Taphouse, 109
Kito's Kave, 24
Klondike Mike's Saloon, 134
Knik Bar, 146
Koots, 78

L
Last Hook Off, 220
Linwood Bar, 128
Longhorn Saloon, 157
Lucky Lady Pub, 35

M
Mad Myrna's, 71
Manley Roadhouse, 191
Marine Bar, 21
Maverick Saloon, 104
Mecca Bar , 166
Mecca Lounge, 208
Midnite Mine, 169
Monroe's Monderosa, 177
Moochers Bar, 170

Index of the Notorious Bars

Moosehead Saloon, 135
Mug-Shot Saloon, 144

O
Office Bar, The, 31

P
Palmer Bar, 132
Panhandle Bar, 67
Pioneer Bar (Anchorage), 60
Pioneer Bar (Haines), 51
Pioneer Bar (Sitka), 27
Pioneer Lodge, 150
Place, The, 112
Polar Bar (Anchorage), 69
Polar Bar (Nome), 236
Potlatch Bar, 8
Powder House Bar and Grill, 142

Q
Que' Ana Bar, 120

R
Rayme's Bar, 19
Red Dog Saloon, 32
Red Onion Saloon, 53
Reilly's Irish Pub, 76
Rendezvous, The, 210
Rose's Bar & Grill, 29

S
Safety Roadhouse, 238
Salty Dawg Saloon, 126
Sand Point Tavern, 219

Sandbar, The, 45
Sea Inn, 228
Silver Fox Inn, 148
Skinny Dick's Halfway Inn, 174
Sourdough Bar, 5
Sportsman's Inn, 98
Squirez, 46

T
Talkeetna Inn, 154
Time Out Lounge, 84
Tips Bar, 130
Tony's Bar (Kodiak), 205
Tony's Bar (Seward), 100
Totem Bar (Ketchikan), 6
Totem Bar (Wrangell), 17
Triangle Club, 39
Trophy Lodge, 185
Tug Bar, 147
Tustumena Lodge, 118

V
Vagabond Inn, 111
Van's Dive Bar, 72
Village Bar, 207

W
Willow Tree, 229

Y
Yukon Bar, 102
Yukon Inn, 193

www.ingramcontent.com/pod-product-compliance
Lightning Source LLC
Chambersburg PA
CBHW011349070526
44585CB00023B/2517